ALSO BY GEOFF DYER

Otherwise Known as the Human Condition:
Selected Essays and Reviews (United States only)

Working the Room: Essays and Reviews 1999–2010

Jeff in Venice, Death in Varanasi

The Ongoing Moment

Yoga for People Who Can't Be Bothered to Do It

Anglo-English Attitudes:
Essays, Reviews and Misadventures 1984–99

Paris Trance

Out of Sheer Rage

The Missing of the Somme

But Beautiful

The Colour of Memory

Ways of Telling: The Work of John Berger

ZONA

ZONA

GEOFF DYER

PANTHEON BOOKS

NEW YORK

Pantheon Books and colophon are
registered trademarks of Random House, Inc.

A portion of this book was originally published in
the *Guardian,* London.

Library of Congress Cataloging-in-Publication Data
Dyer, Geoff.
Zona / Geoff Dyer.
p. cm.
ISBN 978-0-307-37738-8
1. Stalker (motion picture).   I. Title.
PN1997.S6577D94 2011   791.43—dc22   2011011727

www.pantheonbooks.com

Jacket image from the film *Stalker,* Andrei Tarkovsky, director, 1979.
Reproduced by permission of Mosfilm Cinema Concern.
Jacket design by Linda Huang
Book design by M. Kristen Bearse

Printed in the United States of America
First United States Edition
2 4 6 8 9 7 5 3 1

TO REBECCA

I watched the film until the film itself became a kind of blindness.

—G. C. Waldrep, 'D. W. Griffith at Gettysburg'

After all, the best way of talking about what you love is to speak of it lightly.

—Albert Camus, 'A Short Guide to
Towns Without a Past'

ONE

AN EMPTY BAR, possibly not even open, with a single table, no bigger than a small round table, but higher, the sort you lean against—there are no stools—while you stand and drink. If floorboards could speak these look like they could tell a tale or two, though the tales would turn out to be one and the same, ending with the same old lament (after a few drinks people think they can walk all over me), not just in terms of what happens here but in bars the world over. We are, in other words, already in a realm of universal truth. The barman comes in from the back—he's wearing a white barman's jacket—lights a cigarette and turns on the lights, two fluorescent tubes, one of which doesn't work properly: it flickers. He looks at the flickering light. You can see him thinking, 'That needs fixing', which is not the same thing at all as 'I'll fix that today', but which is very nearly the same as 'It'll never be fixed.' Daily life is full of these small repeated astonishments, hopes (that it might somehow have fixed itself overnight) and resignations (it hasn't and won't).

A tall man—a customer!—enters the bar, puts his knapsack under the table, the small round table you lean
against while drinking. He's tall but not young, bald-
ing, obviously not a terrorist, and there's no way that his
knapsack could contain a bomb, but this unremarkable
action—putting a knapsack under the table in a bar—is
not one that can now go unremarked, especially by someone who first saw *Stalker* (on Sunday, February 8, 1981)
shortly after seeing *Battle of Algiers*. He orders something
from the barman. The fact that the barman's jacket is
white emphasizes how not terribly clean it is. Although
it's a jacket it also serves as a towel, possibly as a dishcloth,
and maybe as a hankie too. The whole place looks like
it could be dirty but it's too dingy to tell and the credits
in yellow Russian letters—sci-fi Cyrillic—do not exactly
clarify the situation.

It's the kind of bar men meet in prior to a bank job that
is destined to go horribly wrong, and the barman is the
type to take no notice of anything that's not his business
and the more things that are not his business the better it
is for him, even if it means that business is so slow as to
be almost nonexistent. Far as he's concerned, long as he's
here, minding his own business and wearing his grubby

barman's jacket, he's doing his job, and if no one comes and no one wants anything and nothing needs doing (the wonky light can wait, as can most things) it's all the same to him. Still smoking, he trudges over with a coffeepot (he's one of those barmen who has the knack of imbuing the simplest task with grudge, making it feel like one of the labours of a minimum-wage Hercules), pours some coffee for the stranger, goes out back again and leaves him to it, to his coffee, to his sipping and waiting. Of that there can be no doubt: the stranger is definitely waiting for something or someone.

A CAPTION: some kind of meteorite or alien visitation has led to the creation of a miracle: the Zone. Troops were sent in and never returned. It was surrounded by barbed wire and a police cordon. . . .

This caption was added at the behest of the studio, Mosfilm, who wanted to stress the fantastical nature of the Zone (where the subsequent action will be set). They also wanted to make sure that the 'bourgeois' country where all this happened could not be identified with the USSR. Hence this mysterious business of the Zone all happened—according to the caption—'in our small country', which put everyone off the scent because the USSR, as we all know, covered a very large area and Russia was (still is) huge too. 'Russia . . .', I can hear Laurence Olivier saying it now, in the Barbarossa episode of *The World at War*. 'The boundless motherland of Russia.' Faced with the German invasion of 1941, Russians fell back on the traditional strategy, the strategy that had done for Napoleon and would do for Hitler too: 'Trade space for time', a message Tarkovsky took to heart.

THE SOUND OF WATER DRIPPING. We peer through an interior set of doors, into a room. In film-script shorthand 'Int' means Interior and 'Ext' Exterior. This is a kind of 'Super-Int' or 'Int-int'. Inside already, the camera inches deeper inside. It's as if Tarkovsky has started where Antonioni left off in the famous inside-out shot at the end of *The Passenger* and taken it a stage further: inside-*in*. As slow as that—but without the colour. Antonioni's earlier *Red Desert* (1964) would, as the title suggests, be unimaginable without the colour. The colour—Monica

Vitti's green coat—is what makes it wonderful but for the thirty-four-year-old Tarkovsky, interviewed in 1966, the year he completed his second feature, *Andrei Rublev,* it was 'the worst of his films after *The Cry.*' *Because* of the colour, because Antonioni got so seduced by 'Monica Vitti's red hair against the mists', because 'the colour has killed the feeling of truth.' Well. This takes a bit of chewing and digesting. Take away the colour and what are you left with? You're left with *L'Avventura,* I suppose (also with Monica Vitti), and you're so bored you long for colour, for something to make time pass or to stop you minding that it's not passing. Since we're speaking about truth and how it feels, I feel honour bound to admit that *L'Avventura* is the nearest I have ever come to pure cinematic agony. I saw it one summer, in a tiny cinema in the Fifth Arrondissement of Paris where the screen was no bigger than a big telly. (A black-and-white film, in Italian, with French subtitles, in Paris, in August, in my late twenties: a case study in loneliness.) The only way I was able to get through it was by saying to myself *I can't bear this for another second,* even though there was not actually such a thing as a second in *L'Avventura.* A minute was the minimum increment of temporal measurement. Every second lasted a minute, every minute lasted an hour, and an hour a year, and so on. Trade time for a bigger unit of time. When I finally emerged into the Parisian twilight I was in my early thirties.*

Even to describe the black-and-white of *Stalker* as black-and-white is to tint what we're seeing with an inappropriate suggestion of the rainbow. Technically this concentrated sepia was achieved by filming in colour and printing in black-and-white. The result is a kind of sub-monochrome in which the spectrum has been so compressed that it might turn out to be a source of energy, like oil and almost as dark, but with a gold sheen too. As well as the dripping there is a certain amount of creaking

---

* There's a wonderful moment in *Tempo di Viaggio,* the documentary Tarkovsky made about his time in Italy, researching what would become *Nostalghia* with scriptwriter Tonino Guerra. The two of them are sitting there, chatting. The phone rings and Guerra answers: 'Si. . . . Oh, Michelangelo . . .' Antonioni has called up for a chat! It's the twentieth-century, cinematic equivalent of those entries in the Goncourts' *Journals:* 'A ring at the door. It was Flaubert.'

and other spooky noises that are not easy to explain. We are in the room now, looking at a bed.

A TABLE, A BEDSIDE TABLE, by definition far lower than the table in the bar. The rumble of some kind of transport causes the contents of the table to rattle. The vibrations are enough to make a glass of water shudder halfway across the table. Remember this. Nothing that happens in *Stalker* is an accident and yet, at the same time, it is full of accidents. Next to the table, in the bed, a woman is sleeping. Next to her is a little girl with a head scarf, and next to her, the man who is presumably her father. The rumble of the train grows louder. The whole place is shaking. It's amazing anyone can sleep through a racket like that, especially as the train is also blaring out a recording of the 'Marseillaise'. The camera tracks across the people in bed and then tracks back, moves one way very slowly and then moves back just as slowly. Antonioni liked long takes but Tarkovsky took this a stage further. 'If the regular length of a shot is increased, one becomes bored, but if you keep on making it longer, it piques your interest, and if you make it even longer, a new quality emerges, a special intensity of attention.' This is Tarkovsky's aesthetic in a nutshell. At first there can be a friction between our expectations of time and Tarkovsky-time and this friction is increasing in the twenty-first century as we move further and further away from Tarkovsky-time towards moron-time in which nothing can last—and no one can concentrate on anything—for longer than about two seconds. Soon people will not be able to watch films like Theo Angelopoulos's *Ulysses' Gaze* or to read Henry James because they will not have the concentration to get from one interminable scene or sentence to the next. The time when I might have been able to read late-period Henry James has passed and because I have not read late-period Henry James I am in no position to say what harm has been done to my sensibility by not having done so. But I do know that if I had not seen *Stalker* in my early twenties my responsiveness to the world would have been radically diminished. As for *Ulysses' Gaze,* in spite of the fact that it starred an implausible Harvey Keitel, it was another nail in the coffin of European art cinema (a coffin, cynics would say, made up almost entirely of nails), opening the floodgates to everything that was not art because anything seemed preferable to having to sit through a film like that, especially since the whole thing could be boiled down, anyway, to a single still photograph—a statue of Lenin gliding along the Danube on a barge, a petrified Pharaoh floating down the Nile of history—by Josef Koudelka.

THE RATTLE OF THE TRAIN subsides and there is just the sound of dripping again and we're back where we were a few moments ago, looking at the bed. The man wakes up and gets out of bed. Unusually, he sleeps without his trousers but with his sweater on. For a long time I thought that American men always slept in their underwear. It didn't occur to me that this was a cinematic convention, something that men did in films so that when they got up in the morning, on-screen, they would not be naked. To sleep without trousers but *with* a sweater does not make sense with regard to any system of conventions. It just seems weird and not terribly hygienic. Another weird thing is that although he is keen not to wake up his wife, he puts on his trousers *and* his heavy boots before clomping quietly into the kitchen, but I suppose his thinking is that if she can sleep through the train going by and the blare of the 'Marseillaise'—to say nothing of the ambient creaking, groaning and squeaking—then a bit of foot traffic is not going to make any difference. It's also possible that she is only pretending to sleep. We see the back of his head. The man—and although we don't know who he is yet, for the sake of simplicity, I am going to introduce a slight spoiler at this point and disclose that he is none other than the eponymous Stalker—emerges from the bedroom and looks in through the doors, as the camera looked in a few minutes earlier, when he was in the bed, the difference being that he is no longer in the bed. By any standards it's a slow start to a movie. Officials from Goskino, the central government agency for film production in the USSR, complained about this, hoping the film could be 'a little more dynamic, especially at the start.' Tarkovsky erupted: it actually needed to be slower and duller at the start so that anyone who had walked into the wrong theatre would have time to leave before the action got under way. Taken aback by the ferocity of this response, one of the officials explained that he was just trying to see things from the audience's point of view. . . . He was not able to finish. Tarkovsky couldn't give a toss about the audience. He only cared about the point of view of two people, Bresson and Bergman. Stick that in your pipe and smoke it!*

THE MAN WALKS OFF to the right but the camera stays where he was, seeing what he was seeing, what he no longer sees—which is his wife, getting blurrily out of bed.

He goes into the kitchen. Turns on the tap, ignites the boiler, cleans his teeth. A bulb comes on. Nice: you know, brighten the place up a bit and god knows it could do with a bit of brightening up. Tarkovsky has always been opposed to symbolic readings of the images in his film but one wonders about the significance of this bulb: has the

---

* Tarkovsky constantly reiterated his admiration for and love of these two, especially Bresson, with whom he shared a special Grand Prix du cinéma de création (for *Nostalghia* and *L'Argent* respectively) announced by Orson Welles, in Cannes, in 1983. Quite a trio. Bresson declines to give any kind of acceptance speech, Tarkovsky shrugs and says *'Merci beaucoup';* neither behaves with any graciousness. Maybe both are a little miffed at having to share the honour with the other.

man just had a *bright idea*? If so, it turns out to be not such a good idea: the bulb flares extra-bright and then goes off completely, as if it's blown itself out. It may not be clear which country we're in but wherever we are it seems that getting reliable lighting might be a problem.

IN THIS INSTANCE, there's a more specific problem, and it's called the wife. Either she was awake all the time, or was woken up by the train, the 'Marseillaise', and her husband's creaking around. She's turned the dimmer into the opposite of a dimmer, into a brightener, has lit the place up so brightly that a second later it's plunged into near-darkness again. Their home could do with rewiring, evidently.

You know that expression 'famous last words'? We are naturally curious about people's last words but it would be interesting to compile an exhaustive list of the first words—not just sounds, actual words—spoken in films, run them through a computer and subject the results to some kind of processing and analysis. In this film the first words are spoken by the wife and they are: 'Why did you take my watch?' Yes, the film's hardly started, she's only just woken up and, from a husbandly point of view, she's already *nagging*. Nagging him and calling him a thief. No wonder he wants out. But of course we're also getting the *big* theme introduced: time. Tarkovsky is saying to the audience: Forget about previous ideas of time. Stop looking at your watches, this is not going to proceed at the speed of *Speed* but if you give yourself over to Tarkovsky-time then the helter-skelter mayhem of *The Bourne Ultimatum* will seem more tedious than *L'Avventura*. 'I think that what a person normally goes to the cinema for is *time*,' Tarkovsky has said, 'whether for time wasted, time lost, or time that is yet to be gained.' This sentiment is only a couple of words away from being in perfect accord with something even the most moronic cinema-goer would agree with. Those words are 'a good', as in 'What people go to the cinema for is *a good* time, not to sit there waiting for something to happen.' (Some people lie outside any consensus of why we go to the cinema. They don't go to the cinema at all. For Strike, a character in Richard Price's novel *Clockers,* a movie, *any* movie, is just 'ninety minutes of sitting there'—a remark that could be taken as a negative endorsement of Tarkovsky's claim.)

———

SHE EXPANDS ON THIS NOTION of time—she's lost her best years, has grown old—while the man is brushing his teeth. As she does so you're reminded again of Antonioni because the plain truth is, she's no Monica Vitti. Frankly, the combination of nagging and permanently faded looks seems like a compelling incentive to leave. She lays a whole guilt trip on him, but the usual terms—you only think of yourself—are reversed, given a kind of Dostoyevskian twist: Even if you *don't* think of yourself . . .*

She begs him to stay but, as she does so, you can see that she knows it's in vain, that he's going—even though he's not actually said where he's going. She says he'll end up in prison. He says that everywhere's a prison. Good answer. But a bad sign, marriage-wise. It would seem that their relationship has reached the point where the

---

* Tarkovsky's wife, Larissa, wanted this part and the director-husband was eager to give her the role. He was persuaded to drop her in favour of Alisa Freindlikh by other crew members, chief among them Georgi Rerberg, director of photography on *Stalker*—initially—and Tarkovsky's previous film, *Mirror*. In making an enemy of Larissa, the seeds were perhaps sown for Rerberg's later leaving the film.

default mode of communication is to bicker, quarrel and contradict each other. It's not a lot of fun, this mode, but it's easy to get the hang of and immensely difficult to get out of once you're in it: a prison, in fact. One assumes the man's answer is intended metaphorically but the film often makes us wonder about when and where it is set, and what its relationship is to the world beyond the screen. *Stalker* was made in the late 1970s, not the 1930s or the 1950s when the Soviet Union was a vast prison camp, when, in prison-camp slang (as Anne Applebaum points out in *Gulag*), 'the world outside the barbed wire was not referred to as "freedom", but as the *bolshaya zona,* the "big prison zone", larger and less deadly than the "small zone" of the camp, but no more human—and certainly no more humane.' By the time of *Stalker,* communism had become, in Tony Judt's words, 'a way of life to be endured' (which sounds, incidentally, like an alternative translation of Koyaanisqatsi, the Hopi Indian word meaning—as anyone who has ever enjoyed a couple of bong hits already knows—'way of life needing change' or 'life out of balance'). *Stalker* is not a film *about* the Gulag, but the absent and unmentioned Gulag is constantly suggested, either by Stalker's zek haircut, or by the overlapping vocabulary. As we will discover, the most perilous part of the Zone (*zona*) is the so-called 'meat grinder', another prisoners' term for the procedures of 'the Soviet repressive system itself.'*

---

* And the Gulag, let's not forget, has its own allure and semiromantic mythology. On a couple of occasions, in Paris, I have attended dinners where the guests included men who had been 'in the camps'. Both had about them the quality of election by experience, were assumed to be in possession of a truth about the toll exacted by the mere fact of being alive—of being born in a certain place at a certain time—in the twentieth century. They had been tested. Something had been revealed or vouchsafed them that was simultaneously beyond comprehension and quite routine. Both of them joked compulsively and had no desire to enter the serious political debates that often raged around the dinner table and which I could not participate in—or even follow—because my French was so poor, but I do remember thinking, when one of the women said that she and her husband were going to have a poster of Lenin above their bed, that that was something so ridiculous, so preposterously French, it might have been a quote from a Godard film, one of the ones he made after *Sympathy for the Devil* with the Rolling Stones, an experience that led

After Stalker leaves, his wife has one of those sexualized fits (nipples prominently erect) of which Tarkovsky seems to have been fond, writhing away on the hard floor in a climax of abandonment.*

He, on the other hand, like many men before and since, is on his way to the pub, making his way through railway sidings, beautifully desolate and puddly, in the postindustrial fog.†

Mick Jagger to remark of the great *auteur*, 'He's such a fucking twat.'

* Cf. the second resurrection of Hari, in *Solaris,* coming back to life, so to speak, in a see-through shorty nightie after drinking liquid oxygen.

† Printed in the *Observer* alongside a review by the film critic Philip French, a still from this sequence was actually one of the things that persuaded my friend Russell and me to see the film in the first place. When I was a boy, growing up in Cheltenham, stills were displayed outside the ABC, the Coliseum and the Odeon as a way of luring you in and it was always a significant moment when you saw the still image in motion. (The ABC and the Coliseum are long gone and the Odeon is now derelict, though I still think of it as the Odeon, just as my parents always

As the man makes his way across the tracks, a voice-over says everything's 'hopelessly boring'—a remark that makes one wonder how quickly a film *can* become boring. Which film holds the record in that particular regard? And wouldn't that film automatically qualify as exciting and *fast-moving* if it had been able to enfold the viewer so rapidly in the itchy blanket of tedium? (Or

---

referred to it and the ABC by their earlier incarnations and names—the Gaumont and the Regal respectively—thereby suggesting that these places were the sites of some kind of mythic prehistory, an impression heightened by the fact that I saw the film adaptation of Erich von Däniken's *Chariots of the Gods* in one of them.) It confirmed that you were within the experience advertised outside, even though it was almost impossible to pin down the precise moment when the still was taken (we didn't realize, back then, that a still was not a frame lifted from the flow of images, but a different, independent entity), or at least the slight lag between 'seeing' the still and recognizing it as such meant that it had morphed into a slightly different image. A still, it seemed, was not still at all, more like the aftermath of a more specific but still elusive tingle of déjà vu.

perhaps one of the novelties of our era is the possibility
of instant boredom—like instant coffee—as opposed to
a feeling that has to unfold gradually, suffocatingly, over
time.) The overheard voice generates some very basic confusion: whose words are they? Presumably they are the
vocalized thoughts of the person—Stalker—on-screen,
tramping across the railroad tracks in the foggy fog,
hands in pockets, looking pretty down in the mouth.

Especially when he sees—and it is revealed—that
the person doing the talking, having the overheard
thoughts, is another man, with a woman in a cute little
fur cape. Uh-oh! The talker is still going on about how
insufferably boring everything is. She asks him about the
Bermuda Triangle. He goes on some more about how
boring everything is, reckons that maybe even the Zone
is boring, that it might have been more interesting to have
lived in the Middle Ages. What does he mean by this?
Is he saying, effectively, that he'd rather have been in
Andrei Rublev than *Stalker*? Which wouldn't make
sense, because he's Tarkovsky's favourite actor, Anatoli
Solonitsyn—and thirteen years earlier he *was* Andrei
Rublev in *Andrei Rublev*! She, on the other hand, looks
like a refugee from the Antonioni set. Not only is she

wearing the fur number and a long dress, they're standing by a convertible—with the soft roof up—and she's
drinking out of a long clear glass, as if they've just
emerged from the place where an orgy seems in the off-
ing but never quite happens in *Red Desert*. They are at a
port of some kind (ditto *Red Desert*). There's a ship in the
background, and rigging, derricks.

It is obvious, from the moment he enters the frame,
that Stalker takes a dim view of this pair, even though the
man says that the woman—whose name he can't recall—
has agreed to come to the Zone too, though, frankly,
she does not seem to be dressed for any kind of expedition. She's excited to meet an actual Stalker—evidently
there's quite an aura attached to this shadowy outlaw
caste—but he has just one word for her: Go. It's a man's
world, the Zone. She gets in the car and, pausing only
to call Solonitsyn a cretin (or maybe she's telling him
that Stalker is a cretin), drives off—with his hat on
the roof. It's the first of several humorous moments in
the film.*

---

* In interviews Tarkovsky often strikes one as a bit prig-
gish but there are occasional touches of comedy in his
films. One of them—*Nostalghia*—contains a terrific joke.

Stalker was not happy about the way this man brought along a woman and he's not happy about the way that the man has been drinking. Yes, okay, I've been *drinking,* the man admits, but I'm not *drunk*. Half the population has a drink, the other half is drunk, he says. Is this an accurate reflection of drinking habits in the USSR? Was it one of the things Tarkovsky came to miss about

---

A man comes across another man, apparently drowning in a slimy pond. He pulls him out, saves him, whereupon the rescued man says, 'What are you doing? I *live* here.' I guess that's what is meant by Nostalghia. Is this joke about Tarkovsky looking back at his time in the slimy pond of the Soviet Union? Having got out of it, having freed himself from the stifling restrictions of its filmmaking institutions and processes, he now looks back on it quite fondly. My favourite comic moment, however, is in *Tempo di viaggio,* when Tarkovsky and Tonino Guerra are scouting locations. They arrive in Lecce by car and the great director gets out wearing a pale yellow T-shirt and the shortest, cutest, tightest little pair of white shorts imaginable. He looks like he's flown straight in from the Castro Street Fair!

the slimy pond of his homeland?[*] A couple of times in his diaries, Tarkovsky talks about getting drunk and 'go[ing]

---

[*] Rerberg's alleged drinking and womanizing were contributory reasons for his getting sacked from the film; Rerberg doesn't deny this, though he does suggest that, as far as drinking goes, he was just keeping up with the director. Certainly, drinking on set was a widespread problem, especially during the periods when something went wrong (something was always going wrong) and there was nothing to do but wait for it to be sorted out. A snowstorm in June threatened to shut down the production completely. Then Tarkovsky announced, out of the blue, that shooting would begin again at seven in the morning. Sound engineer Vladimir Sharun went to Solonitsyn's room to let him know and found the actor and his makeup man 'totally out of it.' The makeup man immediately asked for three kilograms of potatoes so that the peel could be applied to Solonitsyn's face and reduce the swelling caused by 'the two-week binge.' (Not two days, two *weeks*.) The potatoes were procured and the potion mixed. Sharun returned to Solonitsyn's room to find the makeup man flat on his back, and the star applying this peasant version of a Kiehl's product to his face.

on the booze', but Stalker takes a dim view of drinking. At this stage, in fact, apart from the Zone, there's nothing of which he does not take a dim view. The man takes a swig from a bottle; in the other hand he clutches a plastic bag, like a teenager with his stash of glue.

STALKER WALKS UP the steps into a bar, the bar we saw earlier. Relatively speaking, customers are pouring in. Happy Hour in a place that looks like people need it. The windows, like the barman's jacket, could do with a good clean. They afford only the dimmest view of the world outside. Stalker is followed by the man, who treats us to another bit of slapstick slipping convincingly on the steps. It's not just customers—the gags are coming thick and fast now, it's practically Buster Keaton round here, Buster Keaton in his long-lost, social-realist classic *Happy Hour*.

THE TALL MAN, the man we saw in the precredit sequence, is still there, drinking coffee, and the barman is still smoking. Not for the last time we are back where we started. We don't need a sign to tell us this is the Last

Chance Saloon. Chance of getting a decent cappuccino? Zero. Hundred-percent-proof vodka? Now you're talking. Stalker tells the tall fellow, Go ahead, have a drink— but when the other guy produces his bottle (he's brought it with him into the bar, coals-to-Newcastle style) Stalker tells him to take it away. Okay, says the man, in the time-honoured sophistry of the alcoholic, we'll drink beer instead. The barman pours him a beer. Stalker glances at his watch, the watch he's stolen from his wife, a gesture of impatience and anxiety that the audience may or may not share. All the time the barman is pouring his drink the man is holding the glass, eager to get on the outside of what's inside it. The moment the barman has stopped pouring he downs it in one—attaboy!—and by the time the barman has finished filling two other glasses, he's ready for a refill. At the heart of the Zone is the Room, a place where—we will learn later—your deepest wish will come true, but one gets the impression that *this* room is his Room, that his deepest wish is being catered for right here, chain-swilling beer.* He brings the refill and two

---

* A sentiment shared by many men on this thirsty earth of ours. When I was a boy my dad would come home

from work, after the summer holidays, full of disgust for his workmates, who had been on holiday somewhere and had spent the entire time at the bar or round a swimming pool, drinking, either in Spain or some other place where the licensing laws were not as repressive as in England. That was their deepest desire and wish. We rarely went anywhere on holiday because my dad's deepest desire was always to save money and the best place to do this, to avoid the temptations of knickerbocker glories and overpriced choc-ices, was not to leave our home, the room where money came in, very slowly, but left even more reluctantly. (I am aware that this is not the first time that I have referred in print to my dad's fear of the overpriced choc-ice. Albert Camus believed that 'a man's work is nothing but this slow trek to rediscover through the detours of art those two or three great and simple images in whose presence his heart first opened.' This certainly seems true of Tarkovsky, especially in Mirror. In my case, it seems that one of these images is a choc-ice and my dad reluctantly forking out for it. I am being unfair, or at least am referring to choc-ices in overpriced holiday destinations such as Bournemouth or Weston-super-Mare. My father had a friend who worked other glasses over to Stalker and the tall man. He's about to introduce himself, but Stalker (played by Aleksandr Kaidanovsky) tells him his name is Writer and the tall guy's name is Professor (Nikolai Grinko). Ah, hints of the heist here: Mr. Pink, Mr. White and all that: generic code names in the style of *Reservoir Dogs*. Has Stalker been lured back into the Zone for one last job?

Every time I see people drinking in films I am immediately seized with a desire to have a drink myself. Certain countries—that is, the films produced by certain countries—tend to make particular drinks look especially alluring. French films, predictably, make one crave red wine, but whites with a château on the label look pretty good too. Whiskey looks good in westerns. ('Men swaggering into saloons. Thirsty from cattle drives.') Beer looks good anywhere. And not just in films. In most countries of the world, even the shittiest ones, you can generally get your hands on a beer that is, as they say,

---

at the local Walls factory, in Gloucester, who was able to get choc-ices cheap. I asked him once if these choc-ices were stolen—hot, as they say in America. 'It's a perk,' my dad said with a look of immense inward satisfaction.)

drinkable. Speaking of beer, we are interested, obviously, to see if Stalker is going to get one down him. Who knows, perhaps he'll even get his round in? As it turns out, only Writer drinks anything at all. Professor sits with his coffee and Stalker just looks anxious. Writer is the one doing the drinking—maybe he should have been called Drinker—and he is also the one doing most of the talking. When Professor asks him what he writes he says one should write about 'absolutely nothing.' So, a Flaubertian in his way. In a letter of 1852 Flaubert announced his desire to write 'a book about nothing, a book dependent on nothing external, which would be held together by the internal strength of its style, just as the earth, suspended in the void, depends on nothing external for its support; a book which would have almost no subject, or at least in which the subject would be almost invisible, if such a thing is possible.' In this direction, Flaubert believed, lay 'the future of Art': 'There is no longer any orthodoxy, and form is as free as the will of its creator.' Compared to content-driven Hollywood cinema this sounds like a reasonable prediction of what Tarkovsky would achieve in *Mirror* (the film he made before *Stalker*): not a film about nothing, obviously (it could equally claim to be a film about everything), but one held uniquely together by the director's style—'the will of its creator'—rather than by the mechanical demands of narrative or 'the burden of tradition.' Flaubert concludes this interlude of speculation with an observation that could have come straight from Tarkovsky's diaries: 'From the standpoint of pure Art one might establish the axiom that there is no such thing as subject—style in itself being an absolute manner of seeing things.'

Anyway, they're standing round the table in the bar, having a good old chat and a drink, though really Writer is the one doing most of the chatting and all of the drinking—and, in the time-honoured tradition of the drunkard, he's repeating himself. He's going on about triangles again, just as he was with the woman outside, before Stalker sent her packing. Triangles this, triangles that. He wonders why Professor is going to the Zone but then launches into his own explanation of why he's going there, what he's looking for. Inspiration, it turns out. He's washed up. Finished. Maybe by going to the Zone he'll be rejuvenated. Man, I know how he feels. I could do with a piece of that action myself. I mean, do you think I would be spending my time summarizing the action of a film almost devoid of action—not frame by frame, perhaps, but certainly take by take—if I was capable of writing anything else? In my way I am going to the Room—following these three to the Room—to save myself.*

All the time this conversation is going on, the camera is moving in, getting tighter, but so imperceptibly you can't tell it's happening until it's happened, until we are practically leaning on the table with them. Often, in Tarkovsky, when we think something is still it's not; at the very least, the frame is contracting or expanding slightly, almost as if the film were breathing.

We hear the hooting of a train, can hear that lonesome

---

* I had intended breaking this little book into 142 sections—each separated from the one preceding and following it by a double space—corresponding to the 142 shots of the film. That's a very low number of shots for a long film and it worked well at first but then, as I became engrossed and re-engrossed in the film, I kept losing track of where one shot ended and another began. This forgetting or not noticing is an authentic and integral part of watching any film—and this book is an account of watchings, rememberings, misrememberings, and forgettings; it is not the record of a dissection.

whistle blow. So, this grim-looking bar does have several things going for it—if by 'several' we mean 'one', namely proximity to the railway station. The hooting grows louder. Do you hear it? Our train? says Stalker, checking his—i.e., his wife's—watch.* They get ready to leave the bar. No one says, 'Drink up!' but that's pretty much the

---

* We can't actually see what time it is. If we could, then part of this scene might have found its way into Christian Marclay's *The Clock* (2010), a video montage of moments of glimpsed time grabbed from thousands of films. *The Clock* lasts twenty-four hours and is synched precisely so that every minute of screen time—as revealed by clocks, watches or dialogue—is exactly the same as the local time of wherever the film is being screened. Tarkovsky expressed distaste for 'montage cinema', but Marclay's sampled narrative is like an extrapolation of many of the points he makes in the 'Time, rhythm and editing' section of *Sculpting in Time*. (Actually, it's possible that this moment of Stalker glancing at his wife's watch *is* in *The Clock* somewhere—I've only seen about ten hours of the whole thing—floating free of the relentless anchoring of verifiable time as a kind of gestural filler. For the record, I did spot a few bits from *Nostalghia* and *Solaris*.)

idea. The camera continues to move in on Stalker, who says to Luger, the lugubrious barman—a type so strong and silent he could have found work as an actor back in the 1920s, before the introduction of sound—that if he doesn't make it back, to 'call' on his wife. And what? Deliver a message of condolence? Sit there smoking a cigarette, silently? See if there's any chance of her laundering his jacket? After this speech Stalker stares right at the camera. Writer is about to leave the bar, we see the back of his head and then he turns and stares straight at the camera so that, momentarily, in accord with the shot–reverse–shot convention, Stalker and Writer have both stared straight at each other. But it also seems that they are staring straight at us. This is in direct contravention of Roland Barthes's edict in his essay 'Right in the Eyes', that, while it is permissible for the subject to stare into the lens—at the spectator—in a still photograph, 'it is forbidden for an actor to look at the camera' in a movie. So convinced was Barthes of his own rule that he was 'not far from considering this ban as the cinema's distinctive feature. . . . If a single gaze from the screen came to rest on me, the whole film would be lost.' In this case, the effect is to implicate us in the reciprocity of their gaze. We are going along for the ride too. We are one of them.

———

THEY—WE—HEAD OUTSIDE. Stalker is carrying some kind of carry-out and he tramps through a puddle. This is no accident. Whatever else he may be, Stalker is a man with a MacArthur-like indifference to getting his feet wet. They clamber into a waiting jeep. The air is filled, now, with the constant blowing of the lonesome whistle. It is raining and the headlights of the jeep are pure white in the gloom and damp. Stalker is driving. Although we cannot see the rain falling through the air—it is drizzling, not pouring—we can see puddles, rain sprinkling the puddles and the headlights reflected in the puddles, and the jeep driving through the drizzled headlights of the puddles, driving through shrubbery, through damp and gloomy alleyways in which lingering mist still lingers. The jeep is perfectly chosen. No other vehicle could serve as well at this juncture. A Mini Cooper would have established a connection with *The Italian Job* (as *Nostalghia* should perhaps have been called) and the sleek convertible we saw at the beginning would have lent a touch of class and glamour, but the jeep, for all its discomfort, harks back to the Long Range Desert Group, to every movie ever made about the Second World War. It is the most swaggering of vehicles, designed for gung-ho generals (Patton) and fearless war photographers (Capa) and, as such, is immune to traffic regulations and the slow congestion of supply convoys. It is synonymous with pure, rugged and *manly* adventure. They are overcoated commandos, these three (one of them will actually turn out to be an explosives expert), volunteers on a daring raid behind enemy lines, with more than a hint of *Last of the Summer Wine* thrown in.

AS THE JEEP turns a corner they hear the sound of a revving motorbike and hit the deck, the damp deck. On release *Stalker* was billed as a sort of sci-fi film and this is the beginning of the most sci-fi-y sequence in the movie, even if, overall, Tarkovsky was pleased with the way that he'd been able to get rid of most of the elements that made it look like sci-fi, in a way that he had not been able to do with *Solaris,* which remained within the confines of genre (difficult to avoid with a movie set *in the future,* on a *space station*) and was, for this reason, Tarkovsky's least favourite among his films.[*]

---

[*] Steven Soderbergh's 2002 version is obviously and consciously a sci-fi film set in the sci-future. He claimed his

film was not a remake of Tarkovsky's *Solaris* but a refilming of the Stanislaw Lem novel on which Tarkovsky's film was based. There was certainly scope for this as far as Lem was concerned; in his opinion, Tarkovsky 'did not make *Solaris;* what he made was *Crime and Punishment.*' Still, in the very first shot of Soderbergh's film (raindrops on a windowpane, olive green and beigey brown) it's obvious that memories of Tarkovsky's *Solaris* (specifically the transitional shot near the end, taking us back from the space station to earth, of a plant on Kris's brown-beige window sill) are intent on coming (and are intended to come) back to haunt us. The film is a lot better than Tarkovsky loyalists might care to admit and George Clooney is good as always, even though he looks, as usual, like he's starring in a (futuristic) advert for George Clooney. The most interesting thing about it, from my point of view, was that from the start Natascha McElhone looked rather like my wife. After a while this became so striking that I whispered to my wife, 'She looks incredibly like you.' 'I know,' my wife whispered back. This resemblance deepened as the film continued. With every subsequent death and reincarnation of her character, Natascha McElhone came to resemble my wife more and more closely until, about halfway through, it was exactly like watching my wife up there on-screen, constantly getting killed off and constantly coming back with more devotion and more love. Although I was deluded in thinking that it was my wife on-screen, this delusion was encouraged by the film to the extent that I was more deeply implicated in the on-screen drama than I had ever been before. Just as writers sometimes speak of an ideal reader, so, in a way, I was Soderbergh's ideal viewer. There I was, sitting thinking, 'My god, it's my wife', and there was Clooney being told, 'That's not your wife.' She kept reappearing as he wanted her to be, as he remembered her, as he wrongly remembered her. Star and viewer—Clooney and I!—were suffering from the same delusion. This was not vanity on my part, and the delusion was not all-enveloping: I wasn't sitting there thinking *I'm married to Natascha McElhone, therefore I'm George fucking Clooney.* But I wasn't—we weren't—alone in thinking that my wife looked incredibly like Natascha McElhone. We once went to a wedding in the Adirondacks where a fellow guest sidled up to my wife and said, 'I've been wondering all weekend if you're really Natascha

The motorcyclist is a guard, patrolling a perimeter or a premise. He's wearing leathers and a white helmet and looks like a guard from *Metropolis* or *1984*. Inevitably, now that certain seminal dates in the calendar of sci-fi projection—1984, 2001—have come and gone, faded into

---

McElhone.' At least two other people made similar observations in the years immediately following the film's release. We watched *Solaris* again a few days ago, only to discover, predictably enough, that my wife no longer looks like Natascha McElhone in *Solaris*—but then neither does Natascha McElhone. We were sitting near her at a lavish fund-raiser for the Institute of Contemporary Arts in London in 2010 and although we did not chat we were able to have a discreetly good gawp. Natascha McElhone and my wife have both changed, but have changed differently—in the same direction (they're older) but in slightly different ways. It doesn't matter. In the film Natascha McElhone is as she is because that's how George Clooney remembers her and she looks like my wife because that is how I remember her. Only the film preserves that memory of how alike they were, more alike than the two films of the same book.

history, large parts of the genre have acquired an anti-
quarian quality, have become a future-oriented subset
of costume drama. One possible interpretation of this
sequence, then, is that Stalker and his mates are trying to
escape from the clutches of history itself, from the ruin-
ous vision of the future announced by Marx, which, a
little more than a decade after the film was made, would
finally declare itself obsolete and bankrupt.

There follows a cat-and-mouse car chase through
what looks like an incomplete Artangel project in an
abandoned warehouse from back in the days when I first
saw *Stalker,* when there were abandoned warehouses all
over London. I say car chase but there's only one car—a
car that is actually a jeep—and it's a bit confusing in
terms of where exactly Stalker is going or trying to reach.
In other words it's a car chase in classic mode in that it
exists not in order to achieve anything in particular but in
order to bring into existence and be part of the vehicular
ritual called a car chase. While the jeep nips in and out of
all this postindustrial dejection the gates are opened for
the freight train whose lonesome whistle we have heard
blowing. Like Luger the barman, the guy who opens the
gate is smoking a cigarette. He might be Stalker's inside

man, a believer in the Zone who, for some kind of cut, has agreed to help them get through. Once the gates are open and the jeep has slithered through he runs off, to alert the authorities, presumably, so that, along with everything else, Stalker has the possibility of a double-cross to bear. We really could be in a heist movie—a sci-fi heist movie.

The big ole freight train hoves into view, bearing components of an electricity generator or something of that ilk, something huge, state-funded and probably harmful to the environment. The heavy train rumbles to the heavily guarded border crossing. The screen creaks under the weight of everything that is being projected onto it, especially since what is being projected is like a distant memory of the dawn of cinema, of the Lumière brothers and their train arriving at the station in 1895. Bright lights. The guards—dressed like the one we saw earlier on the motorbike—check to see that there aren't stowaways hidden on or under the train. *Stalker* has always invited allegorical readings, and since the film has something of the quality of a prophecy, these readings are not confined to events that had occurred by the time the film was made. As the guards scan the train for stowaways, viewers of a particular political bent might be tempted to regard this train as a precursor of the *Eurostar,* poised to enter the Channel Tunnel, having passed close to Sangatte refugee camp, with the Zone an idealized image of the UK and its generous welfare system: a land of milk and honey with many opportunities for those willing to live in Peterborough and dig vegetables for six quid an hour. According to this reading Stalker is himself an asylum seeker—except he's seeking asylum from the *world.* The irony, as Chris Marker points out in *One Day in the Life of Andrei Arsenevich,* his homage to Tarkovsky, is that asylum and freedom lie *behind* the barbed wire, in the Zone. In a way this is also true of Tarkovsky himself, for while he often felt frustrated by the control exercised by the state over his and others' artistic freedom, in the West a subtler kind of censorship and tyranny—that of the market—would have made it extremely unlikely that he could ever have obtained permission (raised the funds) to make *Mirror* or *Stalker.* (How we loved making this point back in the 1980s!)

There's a brief pause as Stalker waits for the right moment to make their bid for barbed-wire freedom. Writer takes advantage of this lull to get all maudlin. He doesn't really care about inspiration, and doesn't know what he wants or if he really wants what he wants or doesn't want what he really wants, and he doesn't even care if the other two are listening—and who could blame them if they're not?

As the train makes its way beyond the barriers the jeep comes sliding along in its wake, on the coattails of the iron horse. The guards are hardly on the ball but, once the alarm is sounded and the searchlights flick on, they are not slow to open fire. It really is all action at this point—maybe Tarkovsky was right about starting slowly so people who'd come in by mistake had time to leave. There are ricochets and everything. Things get blown apart and the jeep crashes through a pile of crates. They come to a halt in another part of what seems an infinite warehouse complex, though the part they're in seems not unlike the part they were in a few minutes earlier. The air is full of the cawing of birds. Instead of the lonesome whistle, there is the busy moan of foghorns. Whatever else it may be this is obviously a major transportation hub. Stalker tells Writer to see if there's a trolley. In a few minutes we will see that he means a little diesel-powered thing that takes them along a narrow-gauge railway track but at this point the word suggests that they are in one of the world's more decrepit airports or an outpost of Sainsbury's that has long since gone belly-up. Obediently, if rather grudgingly (later it will be all grudge and very little obedience), Writer goes looking for a trolley but finds only a volley—of fire from the guards. He is sent sprawling into a spongy safety net of botany. By this point he is possibly regretting all those drinks he downed before setting out on what is proving to be a quite dangerous escapade, not the well-oiled caper that he had envisaged. The sober Professor says he'll go instead, into another even wetter and more ruined part of wherever-the-fuck they are. Shots are fired at him too but they miss and land in the water, leaving pale oblongs of light—reflections of windows, the world outside—to sway and settle and eventually, after the camera has moved on, to resume their shapely place in the brackish water's scheme of things. Professor finds the trolley car and waves the others towards him, through the water that he's just walked through, the water that is being dripped into by more of itself. You can see why Stalker didn't mind about that puddle outside the bar: they all have wet feet now! Another hail of bullets, but harmless, *Where Eagles Dare*–ish in their harmlessness. They clamber onto the trolley car, hunched and seated, and they're off, the three of them, chugging out of sight, screen left.

———

THERE FOLLOWS ONE of the great sequences in the history of cinema. First there is Writer's head in tight close-up while, in the unfocused background, some kind of landscape blurs past. The camera moves from Writer to Professor (in his bobble hat, the texture of his coat in sharp focus) to Stalker and back as they scrutinize their surroundings with concentration, perplexity, foreboding and, in the case of Writer, a suggestion of hungover befuddlement. These are the faces—the expressions—of travellers anywhere, from Columbus's crew in search of the Americas to tourists in a taxi on their way from the airport to a city centre that they—Writer and Professor at least—have never visited before. They're taking everything in even though they're not sure if what they're seeing is any different from what they've already seen or where they've just been. Frankly, they're not entirely sure that what they're taking in is worth taking in, a feeling we've all had as we make our hyperattentive way through the universally uninteresting, often desolate stretch between airport and the luxurious promise (hotel, cafés) of the city centre. Occasionally the camera permits a focused glimpse of what they are passing through—mist, a brick building, piles of discarded pipes, crates, a river (or possibly a lake)—but even then, even when we can see clearly, we are not sure what we are seeing. Outskirts, periphery, abandonedness. Buildings that are no longer what they were once intended for: sites of decayed meaning that may, as a result, have acquired a new and deeper meaning. It depends. On what? On whether we have entered the Zone yet. Difficult to say as the camera—fixed, implicitly, to the trolley—runs horizontally through this area of in-between-ness and indeterminacy. We are, as Roberto Calasso says of Kafka's *The Trial* and *The Castle,* 'on the threshold of a hidden world that one suspects is implicit in this world.' The threshold is a thin line and it is also ubiquitous. Stalker must know if we are in the Zone—he, after all, has been here many times before. So what are his feelings? His expression of furrowed anxiety, of generalized unhappiness—all the world's a prison— has not changed since the film began, when he was quarrelling with his wife, in his sweater and underwear. What we do see, quite clearly, is the patch of white on the left side of his closely cropped hair: is it the mark of a Stalker, of some kind of election? The insistent, soporific clack of the rails is gradually infused with and gives way to clangy electronic music, moving from the literal noise of mechanical operation to a dreamy rhythmic soundscape. It's stood the test of time, this music by Eduard Artemiev with its Indianish drone of flute and stringed instrument (a Persian tar, to be precise) fed through a synth and washing over the steady—and steadily distorting—clang and clack of the rails. It still sounds far-out, has hardly dated at all. Give it a slight remix, put it through a system with some hefty subwoofers and there'd be more than a hint of Basic Channel or one of those other minimalist electronic outfits about it.

In his poem 'The Movies', Billy Collins says he's in the mood to watch a movie in which 'someone embarks on a long journey, / a movie with the promise of danger.' I like movies like that too, whether the journey is by boat (*Apocalypse Now, Deliverance*), train (*Von Ryan's Express*) or car (take your pick). The idea of the road movie is almost tautologous in that all movies are—or should be—journeys, it's just that some of them are so tedious you'd rather be on a bus from Oxford to London. *Stalker* is a literal journey that is also a journey into cinematic space and—in tandem—into time.

Collins doesn't care what dangers are encountered in

the film he's watching since he will just be sitting there, watching. So they're our representatives, these three middle-aged men, sitting there watching, still and still moving, while the endless grey-black imagery slides past their eyes and into their heads. This long tracking sequence, following the trolley as it clanks and clangs along, is the most straightforward journey imaginable—horizontal, flat, right to left, in a straight line—and full of all the promised wonder of cinema. That's what we are being sold in the trailers that precede what used to be called the 'feature presentation'. Unfortunately this has become some of the most debased wonder in the history of the earth. It means explosions, historical epics in which the outcome of the Battle of Hastings is reversed by the arcane CGI prowess of Merlin the Magician, it means five-year-old children turning suddenly into snarling devils, it means wrecking cars and reckless driving, it means a lot of noise, it means that I have to time my arrival carefully (twenty minutes at least) after the advertised programme time if I am to avoid all this stuff which, if one were exposed to it for the full hour and a half, would cause one's capacity for discernment to drop by fifty percent (or, conversely, one's ability to tolerate stuff like this to increase a hundredfold). It means sitting there shaking one's middle-aged head; it means that one is wary about going to the cinema. It means that there are more and more things on the street, in shops, on-screen and on telly from which one has to avert one's ears and eyes. With television I have my strict rule, a rule applying to Jeremy Clarkson, Jonathan Ross, Russell Brand, Graham Norton and a whole bunch of others whose names I don't even know: I won't have these people in the house. It's not—as Stalker claimed—that all the world's a prison; it's just that a lot of what's being shown on the world's screens—televisions, cinemas, computers—is fit only for morons. Which is another reason why, in the long years since I first saw *Stalker,* I am as badly in need of the Zone and its wonders as any of the three men on the trolley as they sit there and the blurry landscape clangs past. The Zone is a place of uncompromised and unblemished value. It is one of the few territories left—possibly the only one—where the rights to *Top Gear* have not been sold: a place of refuge and sanctuary. A sanctuary, also, from cliché. That's another of Tarkovsky's virtues: an absolute freedom from cliché in a medium where clichés are not only tolerated but, in the form of unquestioning adherence to convention, expected. There are no clichés in Tarkovsky: no clichés of plot, of character, of framing, no clichés of music to underline the emotional meaning of a scene (or, as is more usually the case, to compensate or make good for an emotional meaning that would be absent were it not for the music). Actually, we need to qualify this slightly: there are no one else's clichés in Tarkovsky. By the time of his final films, *Nostalghia* and *The Sacrifice,* however, he is reliant both conceptually and incrementally on Tarkovskyan cliché. Bergman said that, towards the end, Tarkovsky 'began to make films that copied Tarkovsky.' Wim Wenders felt exactly the same way about *Nostalghia,* that Tarkovsky was 'using some of his typical narrative devices and shots as if they were between quotation marks.'* The guru became his own most devoted disciple.

---

* On the subject of quotation within film: an interesting study could be made—in a sense this book is a catalogue or compendium of proposals for potentially interesting studies—of scenes in films where bits of other films are seen, glimpsed or watched, either at a drive-in, on TV or in the cinema (*Frankenstein* in *Spirit of the Beehive; Red River* in *The Last Picture Show; The Passion of Joan of Arc* in *Vivre Sa Vie*). Actually, maybe it wouldn't be that interesting after all; one wouldn't get far without the word *meta* cropping up and turning everything to dust. But,

as it happens, this sequence in *Stalker* is used to brilliant effect in *Uzak* (*Distant,* 2002) by Turkish director Nuri Bilge Ceylan. Mahmut, a middle-aged photographer, is living in Istanbul. When his clodhopping cousin, Yusuf, comes to the city looking for work Mahmut is obliged to put him up in his apartment. They may be from the same village but they're worlds apart and Mahmut is not about to compromise his high aesthetic standards just because a dull-witted cousin has come to stay. So when we see them at home, feet up, watching TV, it's not *Top Gear* or *Turkey's Got Talent* they're watching; it's *Stalker,* the trolley sequence. The two of them are slumped and stretched out in their chairs, in a torpor of concentration and boredom. Mahmut is eating nuts, pistachios presumably. Cousin Yusuf has nodded off. One can hardly blame him; even the most boring night in the village cannot compare with the depths of tedium being plumbed here. Professor, Stalker and Writer are on-screen, on the trolley, heading towards the Zone, faces in tight close-up, while, in the unfocused background, some kind of landscape blurs past. The electronic score echoes and clangs through the apartment. Yusuf wakes up, amazed to discover that he'd been asleep for only a few seconds or, even more amazingly, that after a long nap the TV is *still* showing these three old blokes drifting along the railroad to nowhere. Peasant he might be, but at some level he has intuited Jean Baudrillard's insight that television is actually a broadcast from another planet. The evening, evidently, is not going to improve. He decides to go to bed. They say good night. After a decent interval Mahmut gets up, fetches a video, puts it in the VCR and points the remote. *Stalker* is replaced by girl-on-girl porno. Everything else remains pretty much unchanged. Before, he had one foot on the pouffe, and one hitched up over the arm of the chair. Now he has both feet on the pouffe, otherwise he's stretched out the same way as when he was watching *Stalker.* The only difference is that now, instead of this long magical sequence of three men clanging toward the Zone, we've got a silicone-breasted woman sucking the enormous tits of a *Page Three* model. Upstairs, Yusuf telephones home. After a while he comes down again and Mahmut, who has not budged, who is not jerking off, whose fly is not even open, just about has time to flip to a broadcast channel. The fact that the indescribably boring film they were watching earlier has morphed into comedy is not lost on Yusuf—this is much more his cup of tea—and he stands there snickering a bit so Mahmut flips channels again and comes to a kung fu movie—which is exactly Yusuf's cup of tea. *His* evening has improved after all but Mahmut's has taken a decided turn for the worse: no Tarkovsky and no g.o.g action, just him and his moronic cousin watching a kung fu film. It's late, he says. Let's turn that off.

If you wanted a definition of deadpan you could do a lot worse than choose this sequence to illustrate your point. In fact, thinking about it, this sequence is probably the most deadpan I have ever seen in a film. It's so deadpan that you have to be a real cinephile to find it funny and even then you don't actually laugh out loud. You just sit there on the sofa with your feet up, munching pistachios, watching, snickering. If you laugh out loud it's partly to show you get the joke in all its precise levels of denotation but there's an element of affectation about that laughter; it's one of those laughs that contains the desire to explain why you're laughing, why you're so clever. If I were to make a film I would definitely contrive a scene in which a couple of people were watching a bit of *Uzak*, though probably not this bit. That way I'd really show how clever I was and it would give people in the audience a chance to have a good, third-degree, cinephilic meta-chuckle.

Uzak shows and quotes from *Stalker*. But what about the final shot in Michael Haneke's *Time of the Wolf* (2003)? The refugees from an unexplained, all-engulfing catastrophe—at least it appeared all-engulfing at the time, before Cormac McCarthy's *The Road,* after which most catastrophes seemed rather modest and local affairs; at least people aren't *eating* each other in *Time of the Wolf*—are holed up at a railway station where they hope to be able to stop and board one of the trains rumoured to be heading south. (That earlier, facetious reference to asylum seekers is entirely and unfacetiously appropriate here.) The hope offered by these trains becomes increasingly forlorn as conditions and social relations deteriorate—though the hope of some kind of millenarian salvation grows correspondingly stronger. The film's narrative comes to an end. Then there is a long sequence, shot from a train, of landscape rushing past, speed-blurred in the foreground, unspoiled and apparently unthreatened in the distance. Clouds piled up in a silver-grey sky: a sky with spring in its step. An expansive landscape. Trees, roads and clearings, then more trees and meadow. Deciduousness. A level crossing. The odd road sign and house, but no sign of people or cars. The landscape is pristine but not unusually or ominously so. There is no sign of devastation, though it is possible that it has recently been cleansed, not only ethnically but humanly. It has also been emptied of all clues as to what it might mean. There is no explanation of what this train is or where it is heading. The landscape rushing past refuses to sanction any symbolic reference to what has gone before. Trees and sky are absolutely unimbued. Then black. The end. In keeping with Haneke's rinsed neutrality, one cannot say that he alludes to *Stalker*—that would be to freight the shot with exactly the kind of meaning he has rigorously avoided. But if it is impossible, as the poet Anthony Hecht pointed out, 'to begin two consecutive pentameter lines with the words "After the" without an alert reader saying "Ha! Eliot! *The Waste Land,*"' then it is equally impossible to film anything like a horizontal view of a landscape from a train without a similarly alert viewer saying 'Ha! Tarkovsky! *Stalker.*' In both cases the reaction is—Hecht again—'an index of the authority and duration and resonance' of Eliot and Tarkovsky. Since Haneke is obviously a highly alert viewer, he can allude

We are in no hurry for this sequence to be over with, partly because it's difficult to keep track of how long it lasts. Writer's appearing to nod off suggests that, on this most linear of journeys, we are drifting into nonlinear time, are entering dream-time, but a dream-time where everything, every treasured detail is anchored firmly in the real and the now. This is not like the flashing psychedelic rhetoric—'Beyond the Infinite'—of the closing phase of *2001;* this is strictly *within* the finite; it's just impossible to say how long this finitude might extend. We never know when we're going to die, we learn in *Solaris,* and because of that we are, at any one moment, immortal. I read Stanislaw Lem's novel to see if that line was in the book or if it was something added by Tarkovsky. As far as I could tell—I skimmed—it wasn't there, but years later I came across a similar sentiment in a poem by Auden: 'Happy the hare at morning for he cannot know the waking hunter's thoughts.' What are *their* thoughts, the thoughts of these three men, as they travel into the Zone? Professor and Writer are thinking—wondering—exactly the

to *Stalker* without doing so—and, by the same token, can't not do so.

same thing that we are, the question we asked as children on every journey with our parents: Are we there yet? Is this the Zone? Is this it? That, perhaps, is a question that can be answered only by the questioner, when he stops asking it. We are in the Zone when we believe we are there. The blurred landscape slips and clangs past. What we are seeing may be the external representation of the dream-flecked remains of Writer's sleep, a sleep littered with booze-blurred memories of things he has seen a few minutes or hours earlier: abandoned buildings, discarded metals, the man-made poised to return to the natural. Is anything especially worthy of our attention? Everything is, or may be.

IT LASTS LONG ENOUGH, this sequence (a sequence one remembers as a single take, though it actually consists of five), to lull us into a kind of trance. There then occurs one of the miracles of cinema, one of several miracles in a film about an allegedly miraculous place. It's not a jump cut or fade but suddenly and gently—the clanging and echoey clank of the music and trolley are still on the sound track—unambiguously, we're in colour and in the Zone.* You can watch the trolley car sequence again and again, can refuse to succumb to its hypnotic monotony, and you can never predict where it will come, this moment of subtle and absolute transition. Camera and trolley continue clanking forward for a few moments and then come to a halt. The camera pauses and moves back.

We are there. We are in the Zone.

It is every bit as lovely as Stalker claims—and, at the same time, quite ordinary. The air is full of the sound of birds, of wind in the trees, running water. Mist, muted greens. Weeds and plants swaying in the breeze. The tangled wires of a tilted telegraph pole. The rusting remains

---

* The similarities between *Stalker* and *The Wizard of Oz* have been widely remarked on: Dorothy longs to leave her small black-and-white town in Kansas; a tornado transports her to the magically coloured kingdom of Oz, where she and her companions—Tin Man, Cowardly Lion and Scarecrow—set off on a journey to find the wonderful wizard who will allegedly grant all their wishes, etc. Or so I'm told. I take other people's word for it. I've never seen *The Wizard of Oz,* not even as a kid, and obviously have no intention of making good that lack now.

of a car. We are in another world that is no more than this world perceived with unprecedented attentiveness. Landscapes like this had been seen before Tarkovsky but—I don't know how else to put it—their beingness had not been seen in this way. Tarkovsky reconfigured the world, brought this landscape—this way of seeing the world—into existence. Many forms of landscape depend on a particular artist, or writer or artistic movement to render them beautiful, to make the rest of us see what has always been there (as the romantics did for mountains, or John C. Van Dyke for the deserts of the American West). But it's not only the unchanging, eternal, natural world that needs to be mediated in this way. Walker Evans opened our eyes—Stalker himself will soon use that very phrase of his own teacher and guide—to the sagging shacks, wrecked cars and fading signs of America in the thirties. To that extent Evans anticipated Bresson's reminder to himself, in *Notes on the Cinematographer:* 'Make visible what, without you, might perhaps never have been seen.' A little later Bresson added a medium-specific twist to this ambition: 'Quality of a new world which none of the existing arts allowed to be imagined.' Two related questions, then: would we regard this landscape of fields, abandoned cars, tilted telegraph poles and trees as beautiful without Tarkovsky? And could it have been brought into existence by any medium other than film?

If *Stalker* had not been the first Tarkovsky film I saw I might have recognized elements of this landscape from *Mirror*—the cross T's of the telegraph poles, the greens (made more lush, somehow, by being subdued), the distinction between the man-made and the natural being eroded before our eyes. If I had seen *Mirror* I might have recognized this landscape, these elements, as Tarkovsky-land, might have echoed the first words uttered by Stalker: Here we are. Home at last.

And yet, at some level, I *must* have recognized or at least been familiar with a modest and local variant of this kind of landscape—which perhaps accounts, in part, for why the film has made such a deep impression on me.

There is just one train station now in Cheltenham, where I grew up, but in the late 1950s and early 1960s there were four. One of these, Leckhampton, was only a five-minute walk from where we lived. My father used to take me up there when I was a toddler to watch trains steam in and out. The line and the station closed down in 1962, when I was four. I have no recollection of going there with my dad (only of his telling me that we used to go there) but I have strong memories of heading off to this abandoned, brambly zone to play with a couple of friends, when we were eight or nine. The windows of the disused station building had been smashed and the rain had seeped in; it looked as if it had long ago fallen into decay. (It may have only been three of four years previously that the station closed down but this, to me, was half a lifetime ago.) Faded, rain-buckled, the timetable was still displayed—a memorial to its own passing. An empty packet of Player's cigarettes, the ones my mother smoked, with the face of the bearded sailor on the front, gone to a watery grave at the bottom of a puddle: frog-spawny, rust-coloured, pond-size, cloudy with gnats. The tracks had rusted, were overgrown with weeds, grass, stinging nettles, dandelions. Sometimes we followed them for a while, beyond the ends of the platforms, but never as far as the next station along the line—also abandoned—a couple of miles away, in Charlton Kings.

Here we are, says Stalker. Home at last.

THE ZONE PARTS of *Stalker* were filmed in or near two abandoned hydroelectric power plants—one of which had been partially blown up when the retreating Red

Army was trading space for time in 1941—on the Jä-gala River, about fifteen miles from Tallinn, the capital of Estonia. This was not Tarkovsky's first choice for the Zone. He initially intended to film around an old Chinese mine in the Tian Shan foothills near Isfara in Tajikistan. Apart from the single-line railroad track curving through it this earlier version of the Zone has almost nothing in common with the place in the actual film. It's more like the badlands of Death Valley (where Antonioni got the name for and shot the final scenes of *Zabriskie Point*): devoid of vegetation, pale yellow and desert-dry, stark.* Tarkovsky

---

* Tarkovsky encountered a similar landscape again in 1983, just before the Telluride Film Festival, where he was to be honoured—alongside Richard Widmark—with a lifetime achievement award. Tom Luddy, codirector of the festival, served as a kind of Stalker, escorting Tar-kovsky, Polish director Krzysztof Zanussi and others on a road trip through Utah and Arizona. The otherworldly scenery—especially the mythically cinematic Monument Valley—overwhelmed Tarkovsky, but Luddy's attempted explanations of the geomorphological processes at work fell on deaf ears: such a place could only have been cre-ated by god. Anticipating the speech he would make at

loved everything about the original location, but when an earthquake devastated the region before filming could begin, an alternative had to be found. As Rerberg put it, 'The first stone thrown out of the wall of the script was the location.' Footage exists of the original location: one can see how it might have served Tarkovsky's purpose, though the film would have been quite different, would have lacked the damp, drippy, almost-ordinariness of the Zone in its final incarnation. Alien, unearthly (a word applied to a surprising number of places on earth), it lends itself perfectly to sci-fi but lacks the subtle magic of the more temperate Zone. As such it would have rendered that line of Stalker's—'Home at last'—rather odd.*

---

the festival itself (a diatribe against the idea of cinema as entertainment to which Widmark delivered a witheringly polite riposte the following day), Tarkovsky said that only Americans could be so vulgar and materialistic as to make Westerns in scenery like this; in such a place, he said, one should only make films about god. I wonder, was Luddy tempted to reply, 'But John Wayne *is* a god'?

* Or maybe not. In the years when I used to go to Burning Man in the Black Rock Desert, we were greeted at the fes-

Stalker utters this cosy sentiment after stretching his arms, as though he has been sleeping, like one awakened from the dream of life. But it's not only him: the whole landscape seems to be emerging from sleep, rubbing the mist from its eyes, as if it has been stirred into consciousness by the fact of being seen, appreciated, visited, needed. We have only just arrived and already there is a sense, dormant and untapped, of slumbering sentience about the place. How quiet it is, says Stalker. The quietest place on earth. One sees what he means even though, strictly speaking, it's not quiet at all. There are the sounds of birds, wind, flowing water, sounds that emphasize the lack of other sounds, the sounds that constitute noise, industrialization, cities, traffic, stress. As with the unquiet quiet, so with the solitude: Not a single soul here, says Stalker. What about us? asks Writer, logically enough.[*]

---

tival entrance with the words 'Welcome home!' and tears always welled up in my eyes because it was true, because I believed absolutely in the Temporary Autonomous Zone of Black Rock City.

[*] I am reminded of the time, in Big Sur, when a friend and I were perched on the edge of cliffs, overlooking the

Stalker is overwhelmed by his return to the Zone, struggling to compute and explain the way that it compares with his memories of earlier visits. The flowers don't seem to smell. Partly because—this is Writer again—there's a pervasive smell of damp bog. No, that's the river, says Stalker quickly, like an estate agent assuaging the doubts of a potential buyer. But Writer has made his point: to him, the Zone looks like a bit of a dump. He doesn't feel at all like he's home. On the contrary: at this point, he understands exactly what Heidegger meant when he said that 'the unhomely does not allow us to be at home.' Writer, evidently, is in a bad way. He's one of those people who could wake up in paradise but wouldn't know he was there unless he found something to grumble about. There were flower beds here, Stalker says, but Porcupine trampled them down. (This is the first we've heard of Porcupine, a name which has vague asso-

---

fog-shrouded Pacific. Perhaps the fog sealed in the sound of the ocean below. There was no wind. It was absolutely quiet. We were the only people there until a family turned up and the father, eager to articulate the charm of the place, boomed out, 'Must be real peaceful here!'

ciations with *The Last of the Mohicans* or something like that.) The smell lingered for years after the flowers were gone.*

Why did Porcupine do that? Stalker says he doesn't know but thinks that perhaps Porcupine came to hate the Zone. He's sitting down, doing something while the

---

* This is one of several occasions when what we are hearing and seeing on-screen echoes something from the making of the film. Preparing a later shot, when Writer rejects Stalker's warning and starts walking straight towards the Room, Tarkovsky noticed that a few dandelions had blossomed—if that's what dandelions do—thereby spoiling the look of the scene. Production designer Rashit Safiullin and his team were sent to pluck them out. A simple enough task, except the Zone also had to look like no one had ever set foot there, so they needed to make sure that in the process of plucking the dandelions they left no sign of their own work, no flattened grass or footprints. The dandelions had hardly been obtrusive but even when they were removed so that shooting could begin Tarkovsky was not happy: 'Rashit, the flowers are not here but their presence can be felt.'

other two are shuffling about, having a look around, not knowing what to do. Writer wants to know about Porcupine. He was the one who taught Stalker things, opened his eyes—opened his eyes the way Tarkovsky has opened our eyes. He wasn't called Porcupine back then, he was called Teacher and he kept coming back to the Zone, bringing people here. Then something broke in him. Possibly it was a punishment of some kind.

Stalker asks Professor to help tie metal nuts (as in bolt) to some grubby white bandages while he goes for a walk. The wind moves through weeds and plants. The camera lingers on the wind moving through the weeds and plants, on the weeds and plants as the wind moves through them. Professor and Writer are a little uneasy now that they're alone, but they take advantage of Stalker's absence to indulge in that most unZonely of pleasures: talking about him behind his back. He's different from what Writer thought he'd be. He was expecting something more like Chingachgook or Leatherstocking— from *The Last of the Mohicans*! Classic Zone, that, the way that it either reflects what you have been thinking or somehow prompts you to think what it will soon reveal. I mean, where did I get the idea that Porcupine had something to do with James Fenimore Cooper? From seeing the film many times before, presumably, but this muddling of cause and effect will recur again and again. So Writer was hoping for more of a pathfinder, more of a Daniel Day-Lewis bounding through the Mannly wilderness than this anxious, furrow-browed zek who, in fairness, has cheered up considerably since getting into the Zone. We're learning a lot in quite a short space of time. Stalker was in prison. To be a Stalker is a calling but he has paid a heavy price for his calling. He has a daughter, a Zone victim. And what about Porcupine? Professor has done his homework: one time Porcupine returned from the Zone and got fabulously rich overnight. What's wrong with that?, Writer wants to know. (I sometimes think writers' love of money is purer than that of hedge-fund managers or bankers; only serious writers really appreciate the delicious, improbable perfection of *getting paid*.) A week later Porcupine hanged himself, Professor explains. Ah. The camera is sort of drifting back and forth, not going anywhere or doing anything much and nothing much is happening. The air is filled with a howl, the kind of howl the wind would make if a terrible gale were blowing (there isn't a gale) and it (the wind) was the breath of an animal wounded by what it was hearing, by what was being said.*

---

* Lars von Trier takes this aspect of the Zone and raises it to a Hammer Horror–ish degree in *Antichrist* (2009). The most offensive thing about *Antichrist*—worse than the clitoridectomy, the drill through Willem Dafoe's leg and the blood ejaculating from his dick—was that it was dedicated to Tarkovsky. I couldn't believe it. In the classic *Satanic Verses* style of the offended, I did not need my outrage to be corroborated by actually seeing the film. Then I did see it. And, in its weird, perverse way, amongst all the silliness and nonsense—of which there is a vast amount—the film is, very obviously, a warped love letter to Tarkovsky, shot through with allusions, nods and references. At times it looks exactly like a Tarkovsky film. Right at the start, when Dafoe and Charlotte Gainsbourg—gorgeous to look at but, in this instance, hopeless as an actress—are having sex, there's a bottle falling over and leaking water onto the floor, as in *Mirror* and, less exactly, *Stalker*. But it's when they set out for the forest, to Eden, that they head, unmistakably, into the dense remembered green of *Mirror*. (Actually, some of the CGI scenes in the forest, the fairy tale bits, are maybe more reminiscent of

the enhanced forest of Aleksandr Sokurov's *Mother and Son* than Tarkovsky's almost-ordinariness.) The cabin in the woods, the wind appearing from nowhere whipping through the foliage, the orange bonfire, the sense of a landscape being haunted by memory—all of this is wonderful. Some sequences seem even more specifically allusive: the moment when Dafoe turns to the camera as if alerted either by some unspecified external stimulus or in the midst of some inward realization (pure Tarkovsky, that collapsing of the internal and external), or the sequence when we follow him, in his overcoat, from behind, through the ferns and leaves. These are authentic tributes to Tarkovsky, admiring glances from one director to another. Not that *Antichrist* is any kind of Tarkovsky pastiche; von Trier sees what is special about Tarkovsky but does something uniquely his own. What he does is absolutely repellent and silly—a waste. *Antichrist* is daft in the way all horror films are daft, especially when seen beside the routine horrors of modern life.

In von Trier's favour, if you wanted to mount a case for this as a serious—as opposed to a beautifully shot, thoroughly stupid—film, you could say that this is a trip into a mirror image of Tarkovsky's Zone. Whereas in *Stalker*

The howl dies down and segues into Artemiev's drifty, enchanted electronica. 'This isle is full of noises,' says Caliban in *The Tempest*. 'Sounds, and sweet airs, that give delight, and hurt not.' The sounds in this quietest of places are not simply sweet and, at this point, no one is sure whether they will hurt. They have entered—*we* have entered—some subtly altered realm of consciousness in which the powers of the Zone can no longer be denied, but neither can they be proved. An amazing place where amazement is vain because everything is normal here.

The camera glides over the grass, the tangled wreckage of metal and, as it tilts upwards we see, some way off—a hundred yards perhaps?—a ruined house, an unusual property which, while difficult of access (as we have seen) and in need of extensive renovation nevertheless has

---

the Zone is a place where your deepest wish could come true, here it's a place where your most horrible nightmares will be revealed, your—or Charlotte's—deepest fears, the terrors at the apex of the pyramid of terror described by Dafoe. But I don't want to give *Antichrist* too much credit: it's nonsense, a highly crafted diminution of the possibilities of cinema.

considerable potential for buyers who regard the rest of the world as a prison.

Not that Stalker has any intention of buying, even though it is, in real estate terms, the house of his dreams. He sees it from amid a patch of dense weeds and collapses, first in an attitude of prayer and then on his stomach, into sleep. An ant crawls over his finger. There is no difference between the external world and the world in his head. Everything is reciprocated. He rolls over and, for the first time, the look of anxiety on his face is replaced by the flicker of contentment, even, possibly, of bliss. He has returned to the phenomenal Zone and, in spite of the massive weight of his expectations, it has not disappointed. It is still beautiful. The smell of the flowers may have gone but, unlike Gatsby, who is forced to accept the colossal vitality of his illusion, Stalker is still able to believe, to give himself totally to his idea of perfection. He may not be holding his hands together and muttering verses from some sacred text but for Stalker the rapture he feels at this moment is a form of prayer as defined by William James in *The Varieties of Religious Experience*: the soul 'putting itself in a personal relation with the mysterious power of which it feels the presence.'

It will do no good if I keep saying that *this* sequence is

among the greatest in cinema history, that *this* bit is profoundly moving. Those words serve as running heads for almost every page of this book and they apply to so many parts of the film that, from now on, I will try to refrain from using them. But there is no getting away from it: I find this scene, where we witness Stalker's relief and share his bliss (I have been back to this cinematic Zone many times and have never been disappointed) so intensely moving that I cannot watch it without tears coming to my eyes. I'm worried that I'm overusing this tears-coming-to-the-eyes stuff but these are the facts and the fact of my tears—here and at Burning Man—is proof of the profundity of the experience that provokes them. In *Diary of a Bad Year*, J. M. Coetzee finds himself 'sobbing uncontrollably' when he rereads a passage from *The Brothers Karamazov*. 'These are pages I have read innumerable times before, yet instead of becoming inured to their force I find myself more and more vulnerable before them. Why?' That's how I feel about *Stalker*, so I thought I'd ask that same question, to try to articulate both the film's persistent mystery and my abiding gratitude to it.

WRITER AND PROFESSOR, meanwhile, are not totally convinced. Far from it. Professor (i.e., a man used to lecturing) explains that a meteorite fell here about twenty years ago. Or maybe it wasn't a meteorite. Whatever it was, something happened here to cause it to become abandoned. The paradox of abandonment soon kicked in: anywhere abandoned serves as a magnet. In cities unoccupied houses become crack dens; empty warehouses become venues for illegal parties. Leckhampton station became an unofficial adventure playground for my friends and me. People came here and started disappearing, Professor continues. The authorities surrounded the Zone with barbed wire to stop people coming (again, that mirror image of the Gulag: a place surrounded by barbed wire not to keep people in, but to keep them out). More generally, the Zone looks back to a vision of the future—another paradox—sketched in 1946 by the Swiss writer Max Frisch as he surveyed the devastation of postwar Europe. 'This is what exists, the grass growing in the houses, the dandelions in the churches, and suddenly one can imagine how it might all continue to grow, how a forest might creep over our cities, slowly, inexorably, thriving unaided by human hands, a silence of thistles and moss, an earth without history, only the twittering of birds, spring, summer and autumn, the breathing of which there is no one to count any more.'

Tremors from the future can be felt throughout *Stalker*. In less than a decade Professor's summary of how the Zone came into existence had taken on the aura of a premonition fulfilled, and *Stalker* acquired yet another dimension of suggestiveness: in its foreshadowing of the 1986 disaster at Chernobyl, in Ukraine. Tarkovsky was not only a visionary, poet and mystic—he was also a prophet (of a future that now lies in the past).

The damaged reactor and much of the radioactive material at Chernobyl were sealed in a huge concrete 'sarcophagus'. Nearby towns such as Pripyat were evacuated and a thirty-kilometre Zone of Exclusion was established around the plant. Like Stalker's child—a Zone victim, as Professor explains—large numbers of the children of parents who lived near Chernobyl had birth defects. After the evacuation the Zone of Exclusion was littered with the rusting remains of vehicles that had been used as part of the emergency cleanup. Plants stitched the empty roads and cracked concrete. Trees thrust through the warped floors of derelict buildings. Leaves changed shape. Vegetation clambered up the crumbling walls of abandoned homes. Photographs taken by Robert Polidori of Pripyat and Chernobyl in 2001 (and collected in his book *Zones of Exclusion*) look like stills from a retrospective location shoot from the set of *Stalker*.* Except it might not be quite as simple as Polidori and others documenting a world which had come to resemble a film made thirty years earlier. It could be that the photographers' aesthetic—their tacit sense of what they were looking for—was partly

---

* Rather different but even more extraordinary documentary corroboration of the existence of some kind of Zone is provided by Magnum photographer Jonas Bendiksen in his book *Satellites,* particularly the images from the so-called spacecraft crash zone in Kazakhstan and just across the border in the Altai Republic of Russia. The debris that regularly came crashing from space gave rise to a thriving unofficial business here—in spite of the risks—in scrap and salvage. Bendiksen's most famous—and beautiful— photograph shows two villagers atop the dented remains of part of a spacecraft or satellite in the midst of an idyllic green landscape and blue sky, all snow-blurred by the wings of thousands of white butterflies.

formed by *Stalker,* so that the film has helped generate and shape the observed reality that succeeded it.

Rumours began to circulate that within the Zone there was another place (in any magical realm there is always a deeper recess or chamber of more powerful magic) where your wishes could come true. There you have it. In the most concise form imaginable, Professor has outlined the birth of a myth and religion: a place where something may or may not have happened; a place with a power that was intensified—possibly even created—by being forbidden. That's certainly the view of another professor, good old Slavoj Žižek, who reckons that the cordoning off is the defining aspect of the Zone: 'What confers on it the aura of mystery is the Limit itself, i.e. the fact that the Zone is designated as inaccessible, as prohibited.' In a classic Žižekian bit of reverse dialectics, 'the Zone is not prohibited because it has certain properties which are "too strong" for our everyday sense of reality, it displays these properties because it is posited as prohibited. What comes first is the formal gesture of excluding a part of the real from our everyday reality and of proclaiming it the prohibited Zone.'

Irrespective of how it was created, a cult grew around

this Zone. Special powers were ascribed to it. Did it have these powers? It is not made clear. But the belief that such a thing or place exists can bring it into existence—as with the Unicorn in one of Rilke's *Sonnets to Orpheus:* the animal that never was, but was loved just the same. That love, the love of the people who loved this thing that had not *been,* created a space in which it might be:

> They fed it, not with corn,
> but only with the possibility that it might be.
> And this gave the beast such strength
> that a horn grew from its brow.*

---

* Again, myth and reality have become intertwined in the years since Chernobyl. Freed from human interference animals thrived in the Zone of Exclusion. Species not seen for centuries returned or were reintroduced: lynx, wild boar, wolf, Eurasian brown bear, European bison, eagle owl, moose, beaver, Przewalski's horse (whatever that is). The population of already established species increased. A new generation of trees took root, settled in. The forest surrounded and then advanced unimpeded into the ex-city. With animal and plant life flourishing in this way,

It's a gift, this place, the Zone, Professor continues, diligently tying bandages to the nuts. Some gift, says Writer, hand pressed to the side of his head as if talking on a mobile phone. Why would they give it to us? To make us happy, says Stalker, back from his walk, tail wagging. He's in a really good mood now, smiling, clambering past the rotting telegraph poles (part of one actually falls apart as he goes past). Even a reprise of the spooky anguished animal howl does not dent his good humour. Yes, he's having the time of his life—so much so that, without even checking his (wife's) watch he declares, It's time, and sends the trolley clanking back the way it came, along the curving rails, past an abandoned tanker, back into the

---

the Ukrainian government put a positive—and entirely logical—spin on the idea of exclusion and, in 2007, designated the area a wildlife sanctuary. (Scientists who carried out a census and published their findings in *Ecological Indicators* dispute these claims of increase and abundance. They found a diminution in the diversity and numbers of mammals but welcomed the idea of a wildlife haven as a kind of natural laboratory to further study the effects of radiation.)

mists, into the world of black-and-white, and ultimately out of sight, beyond the Zone, beyond the screen. He might just as easily have announced the opposite—it's *not* time. Or at least it's very difficult to work out how much or little of it is passing. Still, sending back the trolley like this begs an obvious question and Writer is the one who asks it: How are we going to return? (It is only now that I notice that they are literally at the end of the line; the rail, here, is blocked by debris. Either the Zone causes the railway to stop or the Zone begins wherever the railway ends. Either way, the Zone is a place you can't pass through, only ever arrive at.) Stalker ignores the question but it seems possible that a well-read fellow like Writer has come across the answer before, in one of Kafka's Zürau Aphorisms: 'Beyond a certain point there's no return. That's the point that must be reached.' The surprising thing—they've only just got here—is that they've reached that point *already*.

Stalker tells Professor to make his way to the last telegraph pole, by the abandoned car. The camera glides towards the car. Plants sway in the breeze a bit. We can hear the sound of footsteps on grass, can see tufts of grass being flattened at the bottom of the screen, so presumably, even though there is no attempt to visually convey the slight jolt of walking, this is the professor's P.O.V. The vehicle, we can see now, contains the burned corpses of two figures hunched over the rusted remains of a machine gun. Scary. Hint of horror. These, I'm guessing, were some of the troops mentioned in the caption, sent into the Zone to . . . do what? To quell it, as the Soviet tanks did in Prague and Hungary? But what was there to quell? There was no uprising, no people on the streets—not even any streets. Nothing. The mere existence of the Zone was a threat. Through the window can be seen the hulks of burned-out tanks in the distance and, nearby, coming into frame, Stalker, Professor and, finally, Writer. So it was not Professor whose eyes we were seeing through. Or at least if it started out that way then it changed without our realizing. This happens repeatedly. We assume that we are sharing the view of one of the participants only to find that he comes into his own field of vision, thereby creating the sense that there is another watcher. The convention whereby the movements of a potential victim are tracked by a camera pregnant with menace—the camera as stalker—is common to all suspense films but here the movement from participants' subjective view to that of an undisclosed third party creates a disquieting sense of there being an extra pair of eyes. There is never a sense that this is the point of view of an actual person, of someone who is stalking the Stalker: it is like an additional consciousness (that of the Zone itself?), alert and waiting. Perhaps this is what Tarkovsky meant when he said that he wanted us to 'feel . . . that the Zone is there beside us.' In other words, that extra person (that extra pair of eyes) is us (are ours). The Zone *is* film.

STALKER THROWS ONE of the bandage-trailing nuts to indicate the route they must take. The three figures make their way towards moss-covered, rusting tanks, troop carriers and artillery pieces. All of this is observed, roughly, from the window of the burned-out vehicle with the charred figures hunched over the machine gun. Is theirs the consciousness implied by the camera's silent watching and waiting?* Is the Zone a place where the dead

---

* If so, then there is an evocative and extraordinarily apposite account of how this might feel in the testament of a schizophrenic patient, as reported by Merleau-Ponty

retain their ability to observe and to see, a consciousness absorbed by the twitching vegetation it apprehends?

One by one they disappear from view into a dip, first Professor, then Writer, finally Stalker himself. We see, for the first time, that Stalker was right: there really is no one here, not a soul, only this graveyard of long-abandoned matériel, rotting in the grass, in the open air, just that and the breeze and the vegetation twitching in the breeze, watched and watching.

A LONGISH SHOT of the three of them, framed by trees, plants, foliage, heading towards us, towards the place they're heading. For the first time they seem not exactly dwarfed but diminished by their surroundings. The woody sound of a cuckoo, which might be a wood pigeon.

---

in *Phenomenology of Perception:* 'Once I was a man, with a soul and a living body and now I am no more than a being.... I hear and see, but no longer know anything.... I now live in eternity.... The branches sway on the trees, other people come and go in the room, but for me time no longer passes.'

Stalker throws another nut. As a method of route-finding this nut-throwing is a bit puzzling. The suggestion is that they are at the mercy of the nut itself, of where it happens to land, as a gambler's fate is decided by where the ball ends up on a roulette wheel. But unless Stalker is a complete klutz, the nuts always land within a few feet of where he intends them to, so there's nothing random about the route. Maybe this is part of Stalker's skill and vocation: reading the landscape, seeing the signs inscribed invisibly within it—like an old woman divining a future only she can see in the pattern of tea leaves in a cup—working out where to go and throwing the nuts as temporary signposts, signposts that are good for one journey only. Stalker said that Porcupine was the teacher who opened his eyes—opened them, presumably, to the mythic significance of certain places and landmarks, to the events that are indistinguishable from the places where they occurred. *When* did they occur? They occurred here, and here, and here. While Stalker went off on his own to commune with the Zone, Professor told Writer that the meteorite—which may not have been a meteorite—landed about twenty years ago but Stalker's sense of what happened can't be expressed or measured in these units. The story of the

Zone, for him, is like Aboriginal Dreamtime: not a set of events that took place in the over-and-done-with past, but lurking in the permadepths of the present.

Other than the nut-throwing not much is happening. Except the camera is closing in, so slowly and so slightly it makes almost no difference, other than to alert us—even if only subliminally—to the fact that something is always either happening or is about to happen or might happen. The Zone is a place—a state—of heightened alertness to everything. The tiniest movement makes a difference. Any deviation from the route indicated by the chucked nuts, Stalker claims, is dangerous. Stalker here is using the word *route* in precisely the opposite sense of Milan Kundera in *Immortality*. For Kundera a route 'has no meaning in itself; its meaning derives entirely from the two points that it connects.' Whereas a road is 'a tribute to space', a route is 'the triumphant devaluation of space.' Kundera is using the word *route* in the sense of route map (which is actually a map of roads in the sense of highways). The route through the Zone is nothing if not a tribute to space. Be that as it may, Writer, having been initially fearful, is getting fed up with Stalker's nut-chucking idea of route planning. He might be Russian but he is the embodiment of a distinctly English attitude:

fuck this for a game of soldiers! Why can't we go straight to the Room? We could be there in a few minutes. In other words he's impatient with the route precisely because it is *not* a route in Kundera's sense. It's dangerous, Stalker says again. Actually, the main danger seems to be coming from Stalker himself. When Writer starts idly tugging on a tree, vandalizing the place, Stalker (who, let's not forget, had himself damaged a telegraph pole just a few minutes earlier) chucks a weighty metal tube at his head for being flippant.

After this little set-to Writer, naturally enough, is in need of a drink. Stalker, uncharacteristically, seems to want one himself. Writer hands him the bottle but any hopes he may have entertained that Stalker will take a slug, that this might after all turn out to be a pedestrian equivalent of a booze cruise, prove short-lived. The mood of buoyant optimism that animated Stalker after his solitary walk proves almost as short-lived; his face has reverted to its default look of profound dismay, of generalized and specific woe. Stalker pours away the contents of the bottle, a gesture that could also be construed as some kind of *puja:* making an offering to the gods of the Zone, wetting their whistles.

Undeterred, Writer insists on going straight ahead, at

his own risk, with or without a drink. The Room looks even nearer than previously thought: about fifty yards? He strides ahead confidently enough but, when the camera jumps in close, right up to the back of his head, he seems to be moving with considerable trepidation. In its way it's a terrific bit of acting on Solonitsyn's part: rarely has the back of someone's bald head expressed such a rich combination of bravado—I said I'd go, so I'll keep going!—and naked dread.*

Stalker has felt the wind picking up but it is only when Writer is seen from the front, making his hesitant way forwards, that we become aware of this wind. The branches sway and bend more deeply. The breeze is becoming a

---

* There's a lot of back-of-the-head stuff in *Stalker;* maybe Darren Aronofksy got the idea for the opening sequence of *The Wrestler* (2008) from Tarkovsky, building up the suspense because we all wanted to know just how beat up Mickey Rourke's face looked after all those years getting beat up in the cinematic wilderness. It might also be relevant—because of the whole space-time thing—that Einstein said that an infinitely powerful telescope would reveal the back of the viewer's head.

sudden gale. We have seen this wind before, near the beginning of *Mirror*, sweeping past the same actor, stopping him in his tracks as he walks away from the woman he has just met, sitting on a fence. Already sentient, the landscape becomes suddenly animate. Writer insists that the landscape amounts to no more than its physical features, which are susceptible to empirical measurement and conscious calculation—that from here to there can only take so long. At this moment the movement of wind through the trees shows the unconscious making itself felt, becoming visible, staking its claim. There is an abrupt accumulation of noise, the flap of birds' wings. A voice orders, Stop! Don't move! and the camera withdraws, sniper-like, more deeply into the building. Whose order was this? Writer comes scurrying back like a whupped dog, demanding to know who told him to stop. Stalker? No. Professor? Not him either. It's your own fear, Professor tells him. You're too frightened to go on so you invent a voice telling you to stop. That sounds about right, but the thing about the Zone is that it's always subtly reconfiguring itself according to your thoughts and expectations. You want it to seem ordinary? It's ordinary—or is it? And at that moment something occurs to make you think maybe it's not ordinary, whereupon it does something briefly extraordinary. (Or does it?) Whereupon it becomes quite ordinary again. The Zone manifests itself even as it withholds itself—and vice versa.*

One thing's for sure: the Zone has comprehensively disabused Writer of Kundera's distinction between 'the

---

* In 1978, while Tarkovsky was struggling to complete *Stalker,* Kollektivnye Deystviya (Collective Actions) arranged for a small number of visitors to travel to a field outside of Moscow. The otherwise ordinary field had been doubly transformed: subtly, by the expectations, uncertainties, arrangements, and reputation of what the Collective termed 'Trips Out of Town'; explicitly by the banner slung between trees that articulated the visitors' experience of mysteriously heightened ordinariness: 'I wonder why I lied to myself that I had never been here and was totally ignorant of this place—in fact, it's just like anywhere else here, only the feeling is stronger and incomprehension deeper.' The banner was unfurled again—this time with what seemed explicit references to the Gulag—as part of 'Empty Zones', a retrospective of the Collective's work at the Russian Pavilion of the 2011 Venice Biennale.

world of routes' and 'the world of roads and paths [where] beauty is continuous and constantly changing; it tells us at every step: "Stop!"'

Stalker says he has no idea what goes on in the Zone when there's no one here; but as soon as people enter it the Zone becomes a system of traps. (One of the big unanswerables: what is the Zone like when there is no one here to witness it, to bring it to life, to consciousness? I was going to ask, rhetorically, if the Zone even existed in the absence of visitors, but one of Tarkovsky's technical preferences suggests that the answer would be yes. The characters are all the time stepping into shot, into an already established frame: screen and Zone are there waiting for them, watched and waiting.) Stalker puts the emphasis on what we want from the Zone, on the needs it answers. But there is always the latent, unasked question of what the Zone needs from the people who come to it, from us. What use is a miracle if there is no one there to witness it?

Everything that happens depends on us, says Stalker. The relationship between pilgrims—even the most sceptical or outright cynical, even those who don't consider themselves pilgrims—and the Zone is absolutely reciprocal. To be *in* the Zone is to be *part of* the Zone. It may be impossible to tell whether a given action is initiated by people or place but the feeling that the Zone is an active participant in whatever occurs becomes increasingly tangible. Stalker is framed against a green so dark it is almost black—what Conrad, with his irresistible urge to over-egg any and all puddings, would have called an impenetrable darkness. This darkness makes Stalker's face and blue eyes burn more brightly as he speaks. With what? With the intensity of his belief, but also—and it is this which distinguishes him from jihadists and born-again Christians—with the intensity of his despair. The Zone is not simply a source of solace, the heart of Marx's heartless world, it is a source of torment, a system of traps that constantly tests, teases and threatens not just his clients but Stalker himself. No one is immune to the capriciousness of the Zone. And another thing, too, separates him from the jihadists. One of Tarkovsky's strengths as an artist is the amount of space he leaves for doubt. In *Grizzly Man,* Werner Herzog looks into the eyes of the bears caught on film by Timothy Treadwell and decides that the chief characteristic of the universe—or 'the jungley' as he metonymically termed it in *Burden of Dreams*—is 'overwhelming indifference'. For Tarkovsky the artist, despite his Russian Orthodox Christian faith, despite his insistence that the epic scenery of Utah and Arizona could only have been created by god, it is an almost infinite capacity to generate doubt and uncertainty (and, extrapolating from there, wonder). This, it hardly needs saying, is a far more nuanced position than Herzog's. The story of Porcupine, Tarkovsky said later, may have been a 'legend' or myth, and spectators 'should doubt . . . the existence of the forbidden Zone'. So to give oneself entirely to the Zone, to trust in it as Stalker does, is not only to risk but *embrace* betrayal by the principle from which he draws his life. That's why his face is a ferment of emotions: everything he believes in is threatening to turn to ashes, the ledge he clings to is poised to crumble beneath the weight of his need for it, the weight that also supports it.

Another word on that wind, the wind that springs from nowhere: Tarkovsky is the cinema's great poet of stillness. To that extent his vision is imbued with the still beauty of the Russian icons, like the ones painted by Andrei Rublev. But, as he himself explained, this stillness is the opposite of timeless: 'The image becomes authentically cinematic when (amongst other things) not only does it live within time, but time also lives within it, even within each separate frame. No "dead" object—table, chair, glass—taken in a frame in isolation from everything else, can be presented as [if] it were outside passing time, as if from the point of view of an absence of time.' Tarkovsky's stillness is animated by the energy of the moving image, of cinema, of which the wind is expression and symptom. Out of this comes the most distinctive feature of Tarkovsky's art: the sense of beauty as *force*.*

Professor sums up Stalker's little sermon: so the Zone lets the good ones pass and the bad ones die? (Well, it's more complicated than that, obviously, and simpler too.) Stalker doesn't know. It lets pass those who have lost all hope, the wretched, he says in an agony of wretched-

---

* This wind that springs from nowhere, suddenly appearing with a force capable of carrying it across the steppes of Russia: genealogically it springs from the opening sequence of Aleksandr Dovzhenko's 1930 silent Soviet classic, *Earth* (*Zemlya*), a film Tarkovsky watched 'over and over again' without ever being able to explain why it touched him 'so deeply.'

ness, never once realizing that he might (by definition) be among their number. Does wretchedness ever have this capacity to transcend itself? Or is it simply a path to further wretchedness? The fathomless implications of this can be seen pressing down on Stalker as he turns from the darkness and walks into the light, where Writer and Professor are framed against the drifting mist and trees of the Zone.

On the very last page of the postscript to *The Varieties of Religious Experience,* William James writes of people's willingness to stake everything on the chance of salvation. Chance makes the difference, says James, between 'a life of which the keynote is resignation and a life of which the keynote is hope.' Again the impossible paradox of Stalker's relationship to the Zone makes itself felt. The keynote of his life is hope, but the Zone will let through only those who have lost all hope. Stalkers, we learn later, are forbidden entry to the Room. Forbidden, perhaps, by virtue of their belief—their hope—in it.

This speech of Stalker's has had an effect on Professor, who is all too ready to resign himself to a life whose keynote is resignation. He's decided to call it a day. If they reached the point of no return surprisingly quickly it's even more surprising to find that one of them has already reached the point of giving up. Sometimes the two are one and the same; the usual difference is that there's only one point of no return whereas the point of giving up is constant—the opposite of a point, in fact—and can be yielded to at any and every step of the way. You go ahead and I'll wait here, says Professor. Given the awesome publicity generated by the Zone—a place where all your holiday hopes will come true!—Stalker has not proved himself to be a very successful tour operator. Or perhaps he's had the misfortune of lumbering himself with two extremely hard-to-please clients. Either way, both of them have pretty well lost faith and interest in the promised package. (In holiday terms the weather is pretty dismal, would probably have been much better in the first-choice destination, Tajikistan.) Writer seems game to go on even if he is scarcely ecstatic about the prospect, but Professor wants to sit here in this nice little picnic spot with his thermos and his coffee and wait for them on the way back. Unfortunately that's not possible. You don't come back the way you go. (So even if you want to give up you have to keep going; the Zone is nothing if not lifelike.) The only option is for them all to return immediately. Stalker will offer them a refund minus a certain amount for his trouble (strain on his marriage, getting shot at, wet feet and so on). Reluctantly, Professor gets to his feet. Go on then, he says, resigning himself to having to live in hope for a bit longer. Throw your nuts. Stalker does so and they tramp off, screen left. There is the call of cuckoos. The camera stays behind, raises itself up slightly so that, above the mist, we can see the Room, the ruined house, which at this moment—the moment when it has become, depending on your point of view, either impossibly far away or barely worth visiting—seems nearer than ever.

TWO

GLAD OF THE BREAK? Of course you are. Any kind of respite is always welcome: the end of a section or a chapter, even a double space break; at a push, just a paragraph. Henry Fielding likened these interludes to stops at taverns in the course of the long journey of the novel. Even if there are no scheduled chapter stops, even if the whole thing is one long, uninterrupted paragraph (i.e., even if you're reading Thomas Bernhard), you can put the book aside and do something else for a couple of minutes, hours or days.

With concerts and plays the intermission often proves a bit of a dilemma. Yes, you can stretch your legs, but there's nothing worse than scrumming for drinks at the bar only to find that by the time you've got your bottle of Grolsch (a drink you would never order in normal circumstances) the bell is ringing to tell you that the second part will begin in three minutes. How many times have you looked at your friends and your unfinished drinks and unanimously decided that, yes, the first half was great but, frankly, we've had enough of that (the music, the play) and could do with a few more of these (lagers)?

In the case of films, with double or triple bills, a break is an unavoidable necessity. Personally I no longer have the stamina (though, unusually for a man of my age, I do have the time) for the Bergman doubles and Bresson triples I used to be able to chug down in my twenties, so am rarely confronted with this problem of intermissions and whether to stay on for the second half of whatever it was that I'd paid good money to see. In the case of *Stalker* there is no intermission, not even time to go to the toilet, just a rather abrupt end to the first part, a few seconds' pause, and then we're off again with Part 2. But those few seconds are enough to break the spell and make one suspect that there's been a continuity error, that something—even if only a frame or two—has gone missing. For a start it all looks a bit darker, as if several hours have gone by and the long day has waned somewhat. We've adjusted to the pace of the film—walking pace, the pace of three men trudging—and suddenly it seems as if we've had a jump cut, a jump forwards in time. Strangely, and uniquely for a Tarkovsky film, we're struggling to keep up, to get on the bus! There is Stalker with his bandages and nuts, scampering through the abruptly darker forest, but then he's outside some kind of building, calling to the other two to come over.

They're taking it easy outside another building or another part of the same building. Either way, how did they get to wherever they are? Again there is that strange collusion between what is experienced by the people on-screen and us in the audience: it's as if they too have taken a break. They seem to have internalized exactly the reluctance to persevere with Part 2 that can assail members of the audience during intermissions. Writer is stretched out on a moderately comfy bit of stone and Professor has found a nice place to sit. They look like they've just woken up, are actually looking forward to a bit of a lie-in. If Stalker has achieved anything so far it is to have united them in their fed-up-ness. I sometimes think this is the real purpose of guides: to serve as a source of bonding for sightseers obliged to follow and listen to them. My dominant memory of the last time I was at the mercy of a guide—explaining the intricacies of Native American rock art near Cedar Mesa, Utah—is of my companion and me chorusing 'Wow!' in increasingly desultory and unwowed tones. From the point of view of prospective clients an obvious drawback of the Zone is that you can go there *only* with a guide, that you will have to listen to him trot out the same stories and the same gags that he's been trotting out ever since he got the job. With Stalker, though, it's not a job, it's a calling, and it's not gags and joking (as Writer grumbles), it's all sermons and sermonizing.

Professor, looking really tired and stiff, steps down from his perch into what sounds like a huge puddle. But no. We cut away to what looks like a reflection of a giant grey moon, smashed apart by a rock or stone—and slowly reassembling itself while Stalker intones some verses by Tarkovsky's father, Arseny. So far the narrative has been strictly linear, following them step by step: border, trolley, walking through the Zone. Tarkovsky himself 'wanted it to be as if the whole film had been made in a single shot.' But now, in Part 2, we seem to have reverted to the loose, associative structure of *Mirror,* which made much use of the poetry of the director's father's. What's happening?*

---

* What happened was that approximately half of the film had been shot (and two-thirds of the money spent) in Tallinn, Estonia, over the spring and summer of 1977, when it became obvious, in the autumn, that there was a

fault, either with the experimental Kodak film that had been used or with the way it had been stored or processed. According to the sound designer, Vladimir Sharun, this only became evident at a screening attended by Tarkovsky, his wife Larissa, Rerberg, and Boris and Arkady Strugatsky who had developed the script from their own book *Roadside Picnic*. 'Suddenly one of the Strugatskys turned towards Rerberg and asked naively: "Gosha, and how come I can't see anything here?" Rerberg, always considering himself beyond reproach in everything he did, turned to Strugatsky and said: "And you just be quiet, you are no Dostoyevsky either!"' With that he stormed off and was never seen on set again. For his part Rerberg insists that he did not go voluntarily, that he was banned from the set by Tarkovsky. Everyone blamed everyone else, but everyone agreed with Tarkovsky that it was a 'total disaster', that the film was doomed. There were proposals to write the whole thing off as a creative accident so that Tarkovsky could abandon *Stalker* and get on with something else. Tarkovsky refused to give up, kept trying to find ways of keeping the ill-fated picture afloat. His intransigence paid off: after much wrangling and manoeuvring it was agreed that *Stalker* would be a two-part film, that another 300,000 rubles would be found to make this second part even though—it was understood—a portion of this extra money would be needed to cover the cost of re-shooting what had been lost. The hiatus was not without its benefits. Tarkovsky always had 'a rigid idea of what he wanted,' according to Evgeny Tsymbal, 'but that idea changed all the time.' The delay obliged Tarkovsky to clarify what he was trying to achieve, gave him the chance to reconceive the character of Stalker, turning him from a 'bandit' to a believer (a believer, like the director, that in spite of all the setbacks, the film about him would be made, that the Zone would exist). It was also during this interval that Tarkovsky ditched the science-fiction element of the film. More exactly, Tarkovsky manoeuvred Arkady Strugatsky—already worn down and frustrated by end-less rewrites—into proposing that he get rid of the science fiction from his own sci-fi story: 'There! *You* suggested it, not I!', said Tarkovsky. 'I've wanted it for a long time, only was afraid of suggesting it, so you wouldn't take offense.' (In a sense this suggests that there was more than a grain of truth in Rerberg's extravagant claim, in the documentary *The Reverse Side of 'Stalker'*, that Tarkovsky chose the wrong book to adapt in the first place!) And so an entirely new *Stalker* began to take shape. ('Everything is going to be different,' Tarkovsky announced in his Diary.) Stripped to its bare bones, the script became a parable with Stalker as an apostle, a holy fool. A new director of photography, Leonid Kalashnikov, took over from Rerberg but, according to Sharun, 'he could not understand what Tarkovsky wanted from him. Kalashnikov left the picture on his own and Tarkovsky thanked him for such an honest, courageous action.' Tarkovsky himself is more concise and characteristically less sympathetic: 'Kalashnikov refused to go on working and walked out,' he writes in April 1978. 'He didn't have the guts to say anything'. Kalashnikov was replaced, in turn, by Aleksandr Knyazhinsky, who shot the final version. It's impossible to know of the exact extent to which this version of *Stalker* differed from the old damaged and abandoned one (preserved by the editor, Lyudmila Feiginova, in her apartment before she and the film perished in a fire). Tarkovsky's assistant, Maria Chugunova, says that they were 'almost visually identical'. Tsymbal thought that Rerberg's footage was 'extraordinary' and 'included astonishing effects.' Tarkovsky, on the other hand, believed it 'lacked simplicity and inner magic.' Aleksandr Boim, meanwhile, supports Rerberg's opinion that Tarkovsky used the numerous administrative obstacles and technical setbacks as a smokescreen for his own megalomaniacal uncertainties. This perhaps is not surprising—which is not the same thing as saying it is untrue—since Boim was also sacked ('for being drunk'). They were 'lightweight shallow people, with no self-respect,' the pair of them, Tarkovsky claimed in his Diary. 'Childish degenerates. Cretins.' Shavkat Abdusalamov took over as art director but was soon sacked 'for behaving like a bastard', leaving Tarkovsky to credit himself as art director in the finished version. Amid all the upheaval, stress and conflict, Tarkovsky was beset with yet another problem in April 1978 when he suffered a coronary. *Stalker,* he decided, was 'bewitched.'

It may be difficult, with so many accusations, recriminations, counteraccusations and denials, to work out exactly what was going on, but the set of *Stalker,* clearly, was a far from happy ship. As Rerberg put it with characteristic vehemence: Tarkovsky may, ultimately, have got the film he wanted, 'but at the cost of a heap of corpses and triple retakes.' As is often the case in the midst of much acrimony, there is a pocket of agreement here; after the

———

STALKER'S POETIC VOICE-OVER continues as the unexplained pale silver-grey circle sways and settles. It is still going on as he lowers himself through the hole in a wall—an abandoned window—and squeezes round the edge of the wall, clinging to it as though on a narrow ledge over a thousand-foot drop. There's a touch of Nosferatu about his expression, the teeth-bared concentration with which he traverses the decrepit remains of what might once have been a half-decent climbing wall. Strength is a terrible thing, we hear, weakness is a great thing. Hmm. In *Enter the Dragon,* a film seen by everyone at my school, we heard that the proud civilizations—Sparta, Rome, the Samurai—all worshipped strength because it was strength that made all other values possible, a counterstatement of belief that was later sampled by the Thievery Corporation on their track 'The Foundation'. Needless to say, Stalker's apparent weakness is insignificant compared with the faith that Tarkovsky

———

disaster of the ruined footage Tarkovsky considered Rerberg 'a corpse'.

GEOFF DYER

believed made him 'invincible'. And Stalker, presumably, draws strength from the memory of the so-called 'beautiful souls' of Russia in the late 1830s and 1840s, men whose personal and political weaknesses seemed intrinsic to their intellectual and moral purity. The obligations of election laid down by one such soul read like a passage from a training manual for the craft of the Stalker: 'You are distinguished from the mass of ordinary souls, and heavenly powers educate and guide you invisibly. For without a certain mood of the soul our science is in vain and our searching unfruitful.'

Stalker comes to an echoey tunnel where he meets the others. They're making good progress, apparently, are ready to go on. Professor is not happy. He didn't realize they were actually continuing their expedition; he thought Stalker wanted to show them one of the local sights—a side trip as they say in the tourism world—and has not brought his knapsack. He has to go back to get it. You can't go back, Stalker tells him. There's no going back, he says, going back to a point made earlier. Professor is insistent. He wants his knapsack. (It so happens that, right now, I identify absolutely with Professor's desire to be united with his rucksack. Six years ago my wife came back from a trip to Berlin with one of those Freitag bags made out of recycled truck tarps and seat belts. Unlike some Freitag bags it was rather plain—plain grey in fact—and initially I was a little disappointed. Over time, though, I came to see that she had made the wisest possible choice and I came to love that bag absolutely. And then, ten days ago in Adelaide, in the course of a long, multifaceted, multi-drinks evening, I lost it, either in a restaurant, at a party, in a taxi or at the gardens of the Arts Festival. No one handed in my bag. It was gone—and is not identically replaceable. Freitag bags now come with a hip fastener, though I could get a reasonably exact match. But it's *my* one I want, that I want back. At this moment, in fact, if I found myself in the Room, my deepest wish is that I could be reunited with my Freitag bag. There is a parable—or maybe it's just part of a stand-up routine—that at the end of your life you are reunited with all the things that you have lost in your life. This lovely idea turns out be a terrible disappointment as you are faced with thousands and thousands of pens and umbrellas, each one a metaphor, I suppose, for the worthlessness of the things by which you set so much value. But it would be nice if, at the end of your life, the locations of where you lost your most beloved ten or twenty possessions could be revealed to you, if you could see a film that showed your younger self walking away from the table at the festival in Adelaide, slightly drunk, while the Freitag bag, discreetly stylish in grey, sat there neglected, unnoticed and mute, incapable of calling out *'Vergissmeinnicht.'* 'So *that's* what happened' you would say to yourself, shaking your head in astonishment, at the simple but profound mystery of loss, on the brink of the most profound and mysterious loss of all, that of your life. And who knows—maybe the revelation of how we lost those treasured things would reconcile us to that other loss in ways that religion no longer can.)

Stalker asks Professor, Why are you so worried about your knapsack? You're going to the Room, where all of your wishes will come true. If that's what you want it will drown you in knapsacks. Good point—though people have set their hearts on stranger, more trivial things. That, in fact, is a version of the good life we are encouraged to pursue, in the misguided belief that an abundance of knapsacks—or iPads or cars or Armani suits—will bring us happiness. (In the case of my Freitag bag, though, it's not that I believed it would *bring* me happiness; it *was* happiness, I realize now, or a component of my happiness, and not having it now is a source of unhappiness.) Still, one sympathizes with Stalker: these clients have got into that complaint-disappointment loop. Everything is turning out badly. Nothing is good enough for them. Especially Writer; ever since he bottled it going towards the Room he's stopped grumbling to Stalker's face and has contented himself with going all hangdog and generally dragging his feet. They are not in the Room yet but they are realizing that one of mankind's deepest wishes is the need to complain, to moan, to be disappointed. Perhaps that's why gods were invented, so you could moan at them for the way things turned out, for things not happening, even, at that relatively late stage of human development (as personified by Thomas Hardy), for *not existing*. Professor asks, How far is it, this Room? In the context of their immediate dispute this could be taken as meaning something along the lines of *Exactly how long will I have to wait till I get all these knapsacks?* More generally, it's a huge and multilayered question, absolutely central to the film. If you go straight, says Stalker, about two hundred metres, but, as we all know, there's no going straight. And the usual measurements of space and distance—miles and kilometres, hectares, acres—are irrelevant. All that matters here is cinematic space. The camera moves forward in what we assume is a linear fashion only for us to discover that we are back where we started. 'The single most important force in Tarkovsky's construction of space,' writes Robert Bird, 'is the motion of the camera.'

Same with time. As one of the characters in *Roadside Picnic* says, 'There really is no time in the Zone.' Stalker and his clients seem to be there for just a day, but once they start taking naps and their dreams merge into the depiction of the actual journey—which is, in any case, all but indistinguishable from a less literal, spiritual journey—time dissolves.*

---

* It was around this point, I think, that when I saw *Stalker* for the third time—at the Academy on Oxford Street, on February 4, 1982—the projectionist got the reels the wrong way round and we suddenly jumped ahead not a few frames but twenty or forty minutes. I was the only one to notice. (Yes, even then I was quite the *Stalker* scholar.) Presumably no one else in the cinema had seen the film before. I dashed out of the auditorium to the ticket desk, explained what was happening and got the whole screening cancelled. My girlfriend and I left the cinema and went to a tea dance (a brief craze) and returned to the cinema two days later and saw the whole film all the way through again.

They prepare to get going, Writer first, followed by Stalker. They're perched, a little precariously, above what seems less like a river than a flow of molten water, polluted by something that makes it more beautiful to look at than simple, natural running water.* The next time we see Writer he is wherever it was they were headed to, bedraggled, mud-smeared and looking more than a little bewildered. He moves off-screen to the right, leaving his plastic bag behind. To our eyes this is an unpardonable bit of littering. The Zone is full of junk: rusting bits and pieces of civilization and warfare but, as they rot and rust, they add to the beauty of the place, whereas this notoriously unbiodegradable plastic bag really is an eyesore. No wonder the camera does not dwell on it but instead drifts right, in Writer's wake, past partly tiled walls, hanging light fixtures and rotting archways through which can

* Vladimir Sharun, sound recordist on the set, recalls: 'Up the river was a chemical plant and it poured poisonous liquids downstream.' This caused numerous allergic reactions among the cast and crew and, Sharun believes, ultimately caused the deaths from cancer of Tarkovsky, his wife Larissa, and Solonitsyn.

be seen—and heard—a brown torrent of falling water. We assume we are progressing but we end up back with Writer again, barely a few feet from where we last saw him. There is no verifiable link—to go back to a point made a few paragraphs ago—between the amount of ground the camera has covered and how far or where it has actually gone. Quaintly, this spot is called the Dry Tunnel, according to Stalker. Very droll. Certainly, by now, the very idea of keeping dry seems laughable as they wade knee deep through running water and make their way through the pouring waterfall. Professor has gone missing—he's gone back for his stupid knapsack, which means he's as good as dead. The other two press on. Impossibly, in the midst of all this watery dampness, the ground pulses with glowing embers as though we are getting close to the burning centre of the soggy earth. Through the swaying water the camera gazes down at the tiled, mossy floor, littered with the soaked, handwritten pages of a notebook or ledger, a rusted machine gun, a syringe.

Freshish out of university, when I first saw *Stalker,* I scanned these objects in the frustrated assumption that their significance—their place in the symbolic scheme of things—would be revealed. But it wasn't. They never mean more than what they are, these things; they are just things—a machine gun, pages, a syringe—lying there while the film of water washes over them and the film of them and the water washing over them washes over us.[*]

---

[*] But maybe my time at university did help prepare me for this aspect of Tarkovsky's art. A famous passage—identical in both the 1805 and 1850 versions—from Wordsworth's *The Prelude* seems very close to what Tarkovsky does again and again (what is *Mirror* if not a visual account of the growth of the director's mind?):

> To every natural form, rock, fruit or flower,
> Even the loose stones that cover the highway,
> I gave a moral life: I saw them feel,
> Or linked them to some feeling: the great mass
> Lay bedded in a quickening soul, and all
> That I beheld respired with inward meaning.

As we have seen, the slow contraction and expansion of the frame creates the impression that the Zone is breathing, respiring, and the passage as a whole fits nicely with the idea of Tarkovsky as a romantic artist, as a *poet* of the cinema. Having compared him with Wordsworth, however, having used that expression *poet of the cinema,* I realize that poets are the only people I want to be poets, that I want poets to be poets only of *poetry.* And Tarkovsky is both more and less than a romantic. The simple things he notices and imbues with breathing magic always remain just what they are. Do they have a moral life? If so it is not one that they are *given* by the artist; it's more like he responds to a tree's tree-ness and a wind's wind-ness which is the only 'moral life' we can expect from a landscape. It is when there is some kind of human interaction with landscape, when the landscape, having been manufactured or altered, is in the process of being reclaimed by nature—a source of abiding fascination for Tarkovsky—that its 'inward meaning' is most powerfully felt.

There's actually another moment in Wordsworth that seems even more proto-Tarkovskyan in this respect. It occurs in one of the draft versions of 'The Ruined Cottage,' when the poet encounters his old friend Armytage, who describes his reactions on coming across the broken walls, overgrown garden and half-concealed well of the cottage and, more specifically, the numerous unnoticed—

———

HERE'S A LUCKY BREAK. Professor has not been gobbled up by the Zone. As Writer announces with unfeigned delight, he's here, waiting for them, reunited with his beloved knapsack, munching cake, drinking warm coffee from his thermos and, relatively speaking, dry as a

---

'I see around me here / Things which you cannot see'—and insignificant objects lying around unused:

> . . . time has been
> When every day the touch of human hand
> Disturbed their stillness, and they ministered
> To human comfort. When I stopped to drink
> A spider's web hung to the water's edge,
> And on the wet and slimy footstone lay
> The useless fragment of a wooden bowl.
> It moved my very heart.

Isn't it exactly this quality of undisturbed stillness that gives Tarkovsky's filmic archaeology of the discarded its special aura?

bone. He's even built a wan little fire. But how did he get here ahead of them, how did he overtake them? What do you mean? Professor wants to know. He just came back here for his knapsack. It's true. They've ended up where they were before all that white-water rafting (without the raft)! T. S. Eliot's overquoted lines about the end of all exploring, how we end where we begin but know the place for the first time, have been proved true in an incredibly short space of time and space (insofar as space and time mean anything in the Zone). Actually that's not quite true, because they don't know the place for the first time, not even Stalker, who looks around amazed, as if he can't believe what he's seeing—especially since the nut he threw to show the way ahead is here, back where they started. And not just the nut: unless I'm mistaken, that's Writer's plastic bag waiting for him. Suddenly the film is all about men being reunited with their bags, either cherished or disposable. (If only my Freitag bag were here too!) Stalker, though, has more important things on his mind, is struggling to process this latest, deeply perplexing bit of data: the fact that they're back where they were however long ago it was that they were last here, wherever that is. The Zone has turned into Thomas Mann's Magic Mountain, where 'the then is constantly repeated in the now, the there in the here.' My god, it's a trap, Stalker realizes. Porcupine must have put the nut there to trip them up, to trap them. It's too much to take in. He won't take another step, he says, stepping away from them, until he's fathomed out what's happening. By fathomed out he means take a rest. According to conventional standards of hiking this seems a singularly inappropriate place to camp: there's hardly a dry spot to be seen. Writer finds a mossy mound surrounded by water, Professor wedges himself on a bit of high ground and Stalker beds down on the edge of what looks like a soaking wet foxhole in a quiet corner of Stalingrad. (No wonder he's coughing.) Writer's delight at finding Professor again is short-lived, or at least it turns quickly to derision at what he perceives as the Professor's motives in coming here, as suggested by what he guesses is in that much-coveted knapsack. Professor is here to *measure* the Zone, to measure a place whose defining quality is its immeasurability, to conduct scientific tests on miracles, to reduce it all to the predictable and quantifiable procedures of science. Writer is one of those people whose default relation to others is to get on their wrong side, to rub them up the wrong way. Snuggled up comfortably enough, Professor responds with a few retaliatory jibes of his own: Writer is a blabbermouth, fit only to daub stuff on public walls. At one level they are now having a more conventional three-men-in-a-Zone-type outing, getting down to the true stuff of male friendship: goading and taking the piss, the British discourse known as banter—albeit in the slightly unusual mode of quasi–pillow talk in which the pillow is a lump of soaking earth and the bed as dank as a river-bed. Their hearts are not really in it, they're all drifting into sleep, slipping into a dream on the fringes of which a black dog comes paddling along the murky river with its linger of mist. The dog stands and looks at us, like it's bearing an important doggy message from the uncon-scious. We slip briefly into swampy monochrome but they're not quite asleep, not yet. Writer asks Stalker—or Chingachgook as he's now taken to calling him—what other people have wanted from the Zone. Happiness, he guesses, looking surprisingly comfortable given where he's lying. Writer says he's never known a happy man in all his life. Stalker might have replied that it takes one to know one but instead, brow more furrowed than ever, concedes, no, neither has he. A strange point to agree on and a little hard to believe—unless this apparent inability to be happy is a distinctly Russian or Soviet indisposition.

John Updike reckoned that America was a vast conspiracy to make people happy. Soviet Russia was perhaps its equally vast antithesis. Writer keeps on: Has Stalker never wanted to visit this Room? Obeying the first principle of drug dealers in any and all films—don't get high on your own supply—Stalker says no. Initially, in keeping with *Roadside Picnic,* Stalker was 'some kind of drug dealer or poacher' but, as the film evolved—especially when its very existence was jeopardized by the catastrophe of the ruined footage—he became 'a slave, a believer, a pagan of the Zone.' So he's fine as he is, thank you, has nothing to ask of the Room in which he believes so passionately, on whose power he has staked his life. He's just tired, whereupon the nice black doggy—so black he is never more than a dog-eared silhouette—comes and sits with him. Writer still wants to talk. What if he returns a genius? Writing comes out of torment, self-doubt. If he returns knowing he's a genius, what incentive is there to write? This is what might be called the Prozac tradeoff or at least a version of the argument often heard in the blissful dawn of the Prozac era, when it seemed likely that Prozac was the formula for universal happiness: surely this would lead to the extinction of the urge to create. Professor begs him to keep quiet, he wants to sleep, but the knowledge that you're keeping someone else awake is one of the incentives for prolonging one-sided conversations like this, even if Writer himself is almost in the land of nod. They're like a married couple who actually get along by bickering (like Stalker and his wife). Neither of them can let it go. One thing Writer does know is that men were put on earth to create works of art, images of the absolute truth—implicitly, works of art like *Stalker*. This is obviously not a universal truth—one could as easily argue that men were put on earth to swill beer, drop napalm on villages or build extensions to their bungalows—but in this context it is persuasive and alluring. One thinks of paintings of bison in the Lascaux caves. Van Eyck. Raphael. Van Gogh. Pollock . . . But you can't stop the clock. The history of art keeps ticking along, keeps being added to, even in a world—as Kundera bleakly envisions it—'where art is dying because the need for art, the sensitivity and the love for it is dying'. It might be a source of regret, but the fact that the history of art includes the likes of Tracey Emin and Jeff Koons undermines Writer's claim except in so far as 'works of art' connote luxury goods of great financial value. (All people think about, Stalker will later lament, is how to get paid for every breath they take.) The conversation drifts on, blood sugar levels have dipped and with the people on-screen barely able to keep their peepers open we, the audience, are hoping that something will happen to revive their energy, to keep us involved. It's the one part of the film that seems to lack conviction and momentum, as if Tarkovsky is trying to make up his mind what to do and where to go next. This is not necessarily a bad thing, strengthening the impression that the film is in some way about itself, a reflection of the journey it describes.

In any case, this slight interlude of ennui is cut short by what comes next: a shot of the muddy expanse of the Zone, dry-looking but rippling—quicksand perhaps.* Whatever it is, this quicksandy stretch of dry muddiness

---

* Like all children, I loved quicksand. In films set in the desert, especially the desert of north Africa during the Second World War, *all* I wanted to see was quicksand sucking jeeps and men into its sucky embrace. Not because I wanted to see people perish but because I couldn't conceive of such a thing actually existing (certainly there was no quicksand where I grew up in Gloucestershire and, for all I knew, none anywhere in England), because it didn't make sense. I loved it, in other words, because it was a

or muddy dryness ripples exactly as it does in the early stages of an LSD trip, when the external world takes on some of the internal rhythms of the body, its breath and pulse. (This, apparently, was from the rejected version of *Stalker,* shot by Rerberg, one of two such sequences to have made their way into the released version.) The first few times I saw *Stalker* were during a phase of my life when I took LSD and magic mushrooms quite regularly.*

---

phenomenon unique to film or television. Quicksand *was* film.

* It wasn't just an LSD phase; it was also a phase of intense cinemagoing and I have no doubt that my high opinion of *Stalker* . . . No, let me rephrase that. The prominent place occupied in my consciousness by *Stalker* is almost certainly bound up with the fact that I saw it at a particular time in my life. I suspect it is rare for anyone to see their—what they consider to be *the*—greatest film after the age of thirty. After forty it's extremely unlikely. After fifty, impossible. The films you see as a child and in your early teens—*Where Eagles Dare, The Italian Job*—have such a special place in your affections that it's all but impossible to consider them objectively (you have, moreover, no desire to do so). To try to disentangle their individual merits or shortcomings, to

see them as a disinterested adult, is like trying to come to a definitive assessment of your own childhood: impossible because what you are contemplating and trying to gauge is a formative part of the person attempting the assessment. Gradually, usually in your late teens and early twenties, you start to watch the major works of the medium. At first it is difficult to make sense of these alleged masterpieces: they are too different, often too boring and challenging. I did the bulk of my serious film-watching as an under-graduate at Oxford, at the Penultimate Picture Palace and the Phoenix, back in the days when there was a late screen-ing every night. By the time I saw *Stalker* I was ready to sit through it even if I was not able to enjoy it. I understood enough—barely enough—of the grammar and history of cinema to see how they were being enlarged, adapted and extended by Tarkovsky. Not that the experience could be confined to the compartment or file called 'cinema'. My capacity for wonder was also being subtly enlarged and changed. At the same time, however, that capacity was also being permanently limited or defined in the same way that reading Tolstoy enlarges and, by so doing, defini-tively limits one's capacity for future enlargement, revela-tion and astonishment in the realm of fiction. Of course you can still enjoy Tarantino after Tarkovsky, can see that he is doing something new; you can see that Harmony Korine is doing something new with *Gummo,* or Andrea Arnold with *Fish Tank*. Of course, of course. But by the time I was thirty, approximately eight years after seeing *Stalker* for the first time, the potential of cinema to expand perception—or at least my own potential to appreciate and respond to, to *perceive* such an expansion—had been so vastly reduced as to seem negligible. For people older than me the expansion had been achieved by Godard; for Godard's generation by Welles or (though this now seems hard to credit) Samuel Fuller. . . . For people younger than me it may well have been Tarantino or the witless Coen brothers. To them Tarkovsky may have the slightly outmoded or taken-for-granted quality that Godard had for me.

Some further refinement—or labouring—of this point is necessary. It happens that the phase of my getting into serious cinema—in my late teens and early and mid-twenties, from the mid-1970s onwards—overlapped with the intensely creative period of what might be called main-stream independent filmmaking, when American direc-tors, having absorbed the influences of the European *auteurs,* carved out the freedom to realize their cinematic ambitions. I saw *Taxi Driver* when it was first released, and *Apocalypse Now* (and *Jaws* and *Star Wars,* which, together with the financial catastrophe of *Heaven's Gate,* heralded the end of this phase).

I saw *Stalker* slightly later but I saw it when it came out, within a month of its release, when Tarkovsky was at his artistic peak. I saw it, so to speak, *live.* And this means that I saw it in a slightly different way from how a twenty-four-year-old might see it for the first time now, in 2012. So much so that the film I saw was slightly different from the one that a twenty-four-year-old would see now, in 2012. Obviously the difference is not as acute as it would be if you saw a band today who were at their peak twenty years ago. The thing, the product, the work of art stays the same but by staying the same it ages—and changes. It exists now in the wake of its own reputation, not quite in the way that *Citizen Kane* does, not only as a monument to itself, but trailing clouds of its own glory. And it exists also in the wake of everything that has come in its wake, both the films that have been influenced by it (that's why *Citizen Kane* is both ageless and incredibly old-looking; practically *everything* seems to have come after it) and the

This shot of the rippling earth seemed a clear indication that what we were dealing with was a trip, that the Zone was a psychedelic place where—exactly in the way suggested by acid guru Timothy Leary—what you experienced was dependent on what was going on in your head. Set and setting. We had excited discussions about

---

ones that treat it with tacit disdain and contempt (*Lock, Stock and Two*—tediously—*Smoking Barrels*). The facts are unalterable. When I first saw *Stalker* it was brand new, the latest thing. I also saw *Pulp Fiction* live, as soon as it came out, but I didn't see it as I saw *Stalker,* when I was at that point of maximum responsiveness or aliveness, when my ability to respond to the medium was still so vulnerable and susceptible to being changed and shaped by what I was seeing. At a certain point, even if you keep up-to-date with new releases (books, records, films), even if you keep broadening your horizons, even if you manage to keep up with the latest things, you realize that these latest things can never be more than that, that they stand almost no chance of being the last word, because you actually heard—or saw or read—your personal last word years earlier.

this, my friend Russell and I, about whether Stalker and his clients ever left the bar, whether they just stayed there, tripping their heads off on fly agaric mushrooms from Siberia. Tarkovsky, it seems, was not averse to such reactions, was pleased 'if at the end the spectator came to doubt whether he had even seen a story.' The ground ripples as if it is not solid at all. A wind kicks up a dust storm, which then seems to turn into a storm of dried blossom, so intense it could almost be snow. (Could that really be what's happening? Could it be *snowing* in the Zone?) The little islands of grass do not ripple. The trees in the background do not ripple: it's just the boggy-looking dried earth that ripples and then, gradually, stops rip-pling. How does Tarkovsky do this, how does he achieve these effects? Or are they not effects? Was it simply luck that he came across a patch of ripply quicksand and then it started snowing where, a few seconds earlier, it had been dusting and blossoming? Is this part of the random magic of cinema that Herzog discovered in a sequence of footage shot by Timothy (*Grizzly Man*) Treadwell? Treadwell plunges into and then out of shot, leaving the camera to record only the wind-whipped bushes and foli-age. 'In his action-movie mode Treadwell probably did not realize that seemingly empty moments have a strange secret beauty,' Herzog explains as the bushes and trees bend and sway in the wind as if in unconscious homage to Tarkovsky.[*] 'Sometimes images themselves develop their own life, their own mysterious stardom.'

It's like a dream but Stalker's eyes are not closed, as if everything we are seeing is an open-eye hallucination.[†] He is so still, his eyes so staring, that he could be dead. He looks, in fact, incredibly like the dead man photographed by Edward Weston in the Colorado Desert in 1937: same hair, same gaunt, anguished features, same stubble—

---

[*] Or, of course, to Herzog himself, specifically the famous epigraph—'Don't you hear the terrible screaming all around you? The screaming that men call silence'—and shot of wheat swaying in the wind at the opening of *The Enigma of Kaspar Hauser.*

[†] I got that phrase from an aging acidhead in Santa Cruz, who first tripped back in the days when LSD was still legal. The difference between acid then and now, he said, was that in its earlier incarnations it produced 'open-eye hallucinations' (as opposed to closed-eye hallucinations and open-eye distortions). An open-eye hallucination: there are worse definitions of cinema.

the only difference is in their surroundings: bone dry in Colorado, rheumatically damp in the Zone. A voice—a woman's or a child's, perhaps Stalker's wife or child—recites a poem that is not exactly a poem; it's a passage from *Revelation* about the moon turning to blood and stars falling from the sky. When I first saw *Stalker* I wondered what this meant and what was going on, in the same way that I had agonized over the Fisher King, *The Golden Bough* and Phlebas the Phoenician in *The Waste Land;* now both film and poem seem to make perfect sense on their own terms even if the exact nature of that sense is as elusive as a fish in water. The camera moves into brown monochrome, the muddy sepia of sleep that is like a dream of death, of the things that are left over when there are no people left awake or alive, a future when it can seem that everything on earth—all the works of art scattered across the great museums—was dreamed by some sleeping consciousness that never quite got round to waking up and resuming work. Beneath the surface of the water are a few fishes (visibly silent in the way that only a fish can be), coins (valueless as currency but, in their obsolete way, priceless) and an image of St. John the Baptist (bearded, kindly, wearing a cloak) from the Ghent Altarpiece by the brothers van Eyck. These sequences, like the green landscape with the wind gusting through them, are quintessentially Tarkovskyan; there's something like this in all of his films: the magic of the discarded ordinary, the filmic archaeology of the everyday.*

---

*In *Mirror* the mother reads a poem by Tarkovsky's father:

> Everything on earth was transfigured, even
> Simple things: the basin, the jug . . .

This is exactly what we get in Tarkovsky's films and in . . . But let's go back a bit, to the moment where Writer says, rather Tarkovskyly, that we are here—on earth, he means—to create works of art. Elide this claim with the lines of Tarkovsky's father and we get something close to the passage in the ninth of the *Duino Elegies,* where Rilke wonders if

> Perhaps we are *here* to say: house,
> bridge, stream, gate, jug, fruit-tree, window—
> at most: column, tower. . . . But to *say* them, you
>   must grasp them,
> oh, to say them *in a way* that the things themselves
> had never dreamt of being.

The poet 'says' these things; Tarkovsky *shows* them, enables us to see them more intensely than we can with the naked, non-cinematic eye. Rilke continues, sketching his poetics of the Zone:

Here is the time of the *sayable, here* its home.
Speak and avow. More than ever
the things that might be experienced are falling
   away, for
what ousts and replaces them is an imageless act.

Tarkovsky is preserving or making visible exactly what Rilke claims is disappearing—ironically, as it turns out, as a result of the amazing ubiquity of the image ('our over-crowded gaze', the poet terms it a few lines earlier). The Zone: refuge of meaning, hope of the unvanished. (This overlapping of Tarkovsky and Rilke is not as arbitrary as it might seem. Having immersed himself in Russian litera-ture and thought after travelling through the land in 1889 and 1900, Rilke, in the words of one commentator, 'came to feel that he could be that country's voice. As he put it more than a decade later: "All the home of my instinct, all my inward origin is there."')

———

JOLTED OUT OF SLEEP and back to colour. . . . The dog is there now, summoning us back to the showable world, the sayable, *barkable* world that we perhaps didn't leave at all, just entered more deeply. Stalker opens his eyes as if returning from the dead, from the dream of life. He begins reciting from the Gospels: and that very day two of them were going to a village called . . . We don't hear the name of the village but it's Emmaus, obviously. Now, one might want to ignore the Orthodox Christian aspect of Tarkovsky but it's unignorable—unignorable but, at least from my point of view, confusable. He himself approaches but they don't recognize him and He asks them why they are sad and one of them named . . . The camera lingers over the face of Professor, just as Stalker is about to pronounce the name *Judas.* Or so I thought because it's all jumbled up in my head, this stuff: vague memories of Sunday school, religious education at school and, more recently (but still a while back), bits from *The Waste Land.* So no, it's nothing about betrayal, it's actually about the Resurrection, the *he is not dead, he is risen* bit. Writer's eyes are open, Professor's eyes are open and neither of them is hallucinating. They really are sitting there listening, both thinking the same thing: Has this Stalker of theirs got a Messiah complex? Not exactly changing the subject but picking up from where they left off before they all nodded off, Stalker reminds them that they were talking about the meaning of life and the unselfishness of art. (Were they? Were we? How long ago?) Take music, for example. It's not connected to reality, is devoid of associations. As he's speaking the camera lifts up from rocks and their emerald-green covering of moss into the glassy grey reflection of the lake. A Sugimoto-esque vision of absolute nothingness, devoid of associations (except, I suppose, associations of Sugimoto), fills the screen until, as the camera continues moving upwards, we see the blurry reflection of the trees that fringe the lake, the still lake, then the trees themselves and the grey sky whose reflection was held by the lake. That glimpse of nothingness unconnected to reality, it turns out, was itself a bit of reality.* And a reminder of how little sky there is in *Stalker*

---

* It was this sequence, apparently, that prompted an official at a Mosfilm screening of the original, damaged version of the film shot by Rerberg to complain that it was

or in Tarkovsky's films generally. He is the most earth-bound, least Shelley-like, of visionaries, interested only in the sky as it is reflected 'in the river, in the puddles.'

There's the woody sound of the cuckoo again. Professor and Writer are listening, spellbound, as Stalker sermonizes about how something in us resonates with harmony, with the unneeded beauty of music. They're not bored or cantankerous kids now, they're entranced, sitting there hanging on his every word, listening to him as if it's the sound of music itself, when there is only the sound of the cuckoo, proclaiming the unasked miracle of its existence.

Not that that makes them eager to sample what Stalker has got lined up for them next: a grimy, slimy, morbid-looking tunnel. Again, one can only sympathize with their reluctance to proceed. The Zone started off as a nice, gentle, benign-looking place but has got progressively scarier and more forbidding with every passing minute. Writer says he doesn't want to go first, and Professor doesn't look too keen either. They draw lots and Writer loses—he'll have to go on point. Having been so contemptuous of Stalker and his nuts, Writer now asks

out of focus: a rather strange complaint since there was nothing on which *to* focus.

him to throw one. He has gone from extreme scepticism to fearful belief. Perhaps this says something about the nature of faith. Maybe there is no belief without fear— fear of the consequences of that belief. Stalker goes one better than chucking a nut, he hurls a huge rock and, as if it's a grenade ('Fire in the hole!'), shuts the creaking iron door to protect them from the blast. No sound at all. The rock has either vaporized in mid-flight or landed on sand so soft there's not even the faintest of plops. This hardly allays Writer's fears as he steps into the tunnel. Stalker and Professor step aside from the entrance of the tunnel as if fearing that any damage coming the Writer's way might end up harming them too. As before, when Writer was making his cynical way directly to the Room, we are right behind him, behind his head as he walks, gingerly, down the echoey, intestinal, glass-strewn, stalactite-adorned tunnel. There's nothing on the walls but damp. It looks like one of the curving corridors of the space station orbiting Solaris, after it's fallen into disuse, been abandoned and left to go to ruin and sublet to the makers of one of the *Alien* sequels. There's no question of a monster or axe murderer leaping out—that is, there's no enslavement to convention—but we are persuaded, by now, that pretty much anything can happen, even if that anything is nothing. It's another of those sequences that seems tacitly about the film itself. Wim Wenders thinks that with *Stalker* Tarkovsky took cinema into 'utterly new terrain' where 'every step could be your last'. Everyone— audience, filmmaker, actors, even the medium itself—is in 'extreme danger at every step'. So Writer is our luckless representative (a Stalker in his way), sent ahead to scout out this 'life-threatening' territory.* He keeps going. One step at a time. We're in front of him now, looking back at him coming forward as he looks ahead, preparing himself for whatever it is he is about to confront. He's not left his fear behind; on the contrary, he is getting closer to its source with every crunching step. The tunnel is leaking like a damaged sub. Water is dripping through the roof and might be coming up through the floor as well. Glass cracks and crunches underfoot. He's in the most danger-ous part of the Zone, the meat grinder, but he could be anywhere:

'The darkness grew loud with the sound of falling

---

* Cf. Bresson: 'Shooting is going out to meet something. Nothing in the unexpected that is not secretly expected by you.'

water, which turned out to be bands of mysterious sub-
terranean rain . . . falling from the confusion of ruin over-
head. We moved through the rain, and fifty yards farther
on climbed on to the dry ground of a catwalk built above
an area of heavy machinery. We paused where the catwalk ended, in a latticework stairs heading down into the
floodwater on the far side. By then we had progressed
deep into the pile, and by ordinary measures were only a
short distance from the main chiller plant. . . . The place
looked like a trap, and dangerous as hell'.

This reads like a passage from a book written by
Writer after he got back: *Zona,* the best-selling, true-life
story of his adventures with Stalker. It's actually from
American Ground, William Langewiesche's account of
'The Unbuilding of the World Trade Center' in the
wake of the 9/11 attacks. Once again, I am struck by the
film's *reach,* its ability to bathe events—both actual and
cultural—in its projected light.

Writer sees something, something—to judge by his
expression—horrible and terrifying. A door, he shouts.
Stalker, keeping well back, tells him to open it. Writer at
this point is, as we used to say at school, bricking it. Whatever lies beyond that door—another of those submarine-

type hatches—could be extremely unpleasant. He draws a gun. A terrible mistake. By drawing the gun he is sealing his fate. Stalker begs him to get rid of it: Remember the tanks! Writer pauses. Perhaps he is recalling the exclamations of amazement—'Bullets just bounce off it!'—in those American sci-fi movies where the monster from outer space is, as often as not, a symbol of the implacable menace of Russians among whose number Writer must, of course, count himself (so that effectively he is his own worst enemy). Accepting the probable uselessness of a weapon in the face of whatever threat may or may not be lurking, Writer drops the gun. Opens the door. There is a chamber full of water—it's like a scene from *The Poseidon Adventure* but set on the *Kursk,* the stricken sub that became the doomed sub. Not just any old water. It looks cold, suddy (as if some of the world's dirtiest dishes had been washed in it), polluted and possibly radioactive to boot. Nevertheless Writer descends the stairs, up to his chest. He's so inured to the soaking conditions of the Zone that he doesn't even take off his overcoat and hold it over his head. He's absolutely drenched. Professor follows but Stalker, worried, now, about what these clients of his might be carrying, asks Professor if he's got something

like that. Like what? Like a gun? No, just an ampoule of
poison in case, he says, descending into the washing-up
water, holding his beloved knapsack above his head like a
grunt carrying his M16 through a monsoon-swollen river
in Nam. What? Did he come here to die, Stalker wants
to know. Professor doesn't answer; he's too busy wading.
He's absolutely drenched too. In terms of who's winning
the Soak the Bloke competition there's nothing to choose
between them. They've both had their Zonal baptism.
Stalker follows, nudging Writer's discarded pistol into
the water, where it will assume the status of harmless relic,
symbol of everything that it is and isn't. Then he's yell-
ing again at Writer, who, having been reluctant to take
the lead, has failed to stop, has marched on into a huge
room filled with hummocks of sand. It's like Walter De
Maria's *New York Earth Room* but made of sand and far
bigger. A nut thrown by Stalker bounces slow-motionly
off the sand. Stalker and Writer dive for cover, hit the
deck, the deck of sand. Writer looks bemused, unsure of
his bearings. A flash of light blinds him. A bird flaps past,
flies deep into this interior meadow of sand and, before
it can land, disappears, is CGI'd (in the days before CGI)
into nonexistence. Another bird follows immediately and

doesn't disappear, just lands like a normal bird would land. That's the Zone for you: completely weird and completely ordinary.*

It was not a case of love at first sight: the first time I saw *Stalker* I was slightly bored and unmoved. I wasn't overwhelmed (to put it slightly stupidly, I had no idea that, thirty years later, I would end up writing *an entire book* about it), but it was an experience I couldn't shake off. Something about it stayed with me. I was living in Putney at the time and one day my then-girlfriend and I went walking in Richmond Park. It was autumn and

---

* Tilda Swinton's character—white wig, white shades, white cowboy hat, white mac—mentions this sequence in Jim Jarmusch's vacuous *The Limits of Control*. She was apparently drawing on her own experiences as a student at Cambridge in the 1980s: 'I saw Tarkovsky's *Stalker,* and there's a scene of that image—of a bird flying through a room of sand. And I'd been having that dream my whole life, or probably since before I was ten. I've stopped having it since seeing that film, but it really blew my mind that someone else would have exactly the same image somehow and put it in a film. That really informed my relationship with cinema: the idea that it *is* what's unconscious.'

a bird flew over the sloping ground towards a clump of trees, flapped and flew in a way that was strangely reminiscent of the way that second bird had flown into this vast room of sand. I wanted to see the film again immediately after that, and since then the desire to see it again—and again and again—has never gone away.* Until now.

---

* I may have wanted to see it again immediately but that was impossible. I had to wait until it was showing at a cinema again. Of course it's fantastically convenient, being able to see *Stalker*—or at least to refer to it—at home, on DVD, whenever the urge takes one. But I liked the way that my visits to the Zone were at the mercy of cinema schedules and festival programmes. In London or in any other city where I happened to be living I always looked through *Time Out* or *Pariscope* or the *Village Voice* in the hope that *Stalker* would be playing. If it was showing somewhere, then seeing it became a priority, an event that gave shape to the surrounding week. Like this, the Zone retained its specialness, its removal from the everyday (of which it remained, at the same time, a part). Getting there was always a little expedition, a cinematic pilgrimage. As was entirely appropriate to the Zone, the film changed slightly, manifested itself differently according to where it

happened to be found: the fact that I was seeing *Stalker* in a tiny cinema in the Fifth *arrondissement* of Paris—the same cinema, in fact, where I had sat through *L'Avventura*—made it a slightly different experience to seeing it as part of a Tarkovsky retrospective at Lincoln Center in New York. But what about the possibility of a cinema as semipermanent pilgrimage site? Bresson believed that the riches offered by certain films were so inexhaustible that 'there ought to be in Paris one quite small, very well equipped cinema, in which only one or two films would be shown each year.' Taking this a stage further, how about a cinema dedicated to showing *Stalker* exclusively? (For a less rapturous take on such a possibility see David Thomson on page 159.)

At various times before the advent of DVDs, *Stalker* was shown on TV and I taped it, to make sure I had a record of the film but, unlike Mahmut in *Uzak*, I never watched *Stalker* on telly. That list of things and people I won't watch on TV does not stop at *Top Gear* and Jeremy Clarkson. It also includes . . . *Stalker*. One cannot watch *Stalker* on TV for the simple reason that the Zone *is* cinema; it does not even *exist* on telly. The prohibition extends beyond *Stalker,* to anything that has any cinematic value. It doesn't matter if the TV is HD: great cinema must be projected. It is the difference, as John Berger puts it, between watching the sky ('from where else would film stars come if not from a film sky?') and peering into a cupboard. I was so unshakeable in this rule, at a time when fewer and fewer classic films were being shown at the cinema, that I was in danger of eliminating much of film history from my life. I would permit us to watch only romcoms at home, films whose defining characteristic was an absolute lack of cinematic value. So we bought a DVD projector and it was wonderful, even though the setup each time we wanted to watch a film—setting the aspect ratio, clambering through the complexities of the menu tree, shifting stereo speakers, lowering the blinds to eliminate light from the street—often reduced me to a state of such fury that the screening had to be aborted. All of this was, perhaps, to be expected. The unexpected problem was that so many of the classic films of the past actually turned out to be pretty terrible. Buñuel's *The Discreet Charm of the Bourgeoisie* and *Belle de Jour* sucked. Godard's *Breathless* was unwatchable, and not only because of the smoking.

After this watch-a-thon, I might never want to set eyes on it again; after this, I might have laid it to rest for good. We shall see. As for the disappearing bird, I now feel that it might have been better if it *hadn't* disappeared, if it had been a regular *flying* bird, not a magical disappearing bird. In fact, I could do without most of the overtly spooky or magical bits of the Zone—that voice calling out 'Stop' to Writer, for example. I am so convinced of the magic and mystery of the Zone that there is no need for it to be anything other than completely natural and normal—though maybe that magic could not have been achieved without things like the disappearing bird. Oh, and the acid ripple of the earth—I would always want that to be there.

Kieslowski's *The Double Life of Véronique* made straight-ahead porn seem tasteful by comparison. Getting through Bresson's *Diary of a Country Priest* was a bit of a struggle too. Still, at least we could watch Tarkovsky. Except *Nostalghia,* a film I saw and was disappointed and bored by when it first came out, was even worse than I remembered it, so bad—*so* far up itself—that I thought it best to leave *The Sacrifice* on the video shop's shelves of memory.

Professor and Stalker peer above the sandy hillocks like they're on a soundstage for a sci-fi remake of *Sands of Iwo Jima*. (Mention of a soundstage makes me realize something that I've been reluctant not only to admit but even—after all these viewings—to notice: that some of these interior sequences in the Zone look a bit too much like they were filmed in a film studio, as opposed to looking like they were scouted out, discovered, chanced upon. They look designed and manufactured, which is to say they look *over*designed.) Writer has suffered some kind of collapse. He's lying in a puddle of water: he's adapted so thoroughly to the idea of never getting dry that he's practically amphibious. Behind him is a round metallic container or drum. He gets up, walks towards it, peers inside, walks back, picks up a rock—possibly the same rock thrown by Stalker, even though, strictly speaking, that's impossible (if it makes sense to talk of the impossible in a realm in which anything is possible) and drops it into this shallow drum. Maybe it *is* the same stone, the stone that makes no sound when it lands, because there is no splash or clang at all, nothing—and then, after ten or twelve seconds, there is an echoey, clanging splash suggesting that the drop is about the height of the Empire

State Building at least. It's only now that something seen earlier makes sense: the splashing moon right at the beginning of Part 2, with the poetry intoned over it. That, presumably, was a view from above of the stone striking the surface of the mercury-water at the bottom of this tube or drum or whatever it is. Given the depth, it's quite ballsy of Writer to perch on the rim of this drum—a drum that is in fact a mile-deep shaft—as if on the edge of a paddling pool made from Meccano.

Writer is by now a wholehearted believer. Dropping the stone—a Professorly experiment of sorts—has proved to him that there are no facts here. It's all someone's idiotic invention—but whose? Well, Tarkovsky's, if one subscribes to the *auteur* theory of cinema, I suppose. Not that Writer is interested in answers to this rhetorical question. He's basically having a good old snivel and, like most writers given half the chance, the snivelling soon takes the form of whining about critics, about how his work has not been properly understood, snivel snivel. What the hell kind of writer is he if he hates writing? A true writer, as defined by Thomas Mann: someone who finds writing more difficult than other people. Not that this is any consolation. Quite the contrary. Writing is the opposite of consolation, it's torment, like squeezing out haemorrhoids, he reckons—a comparison that actually has its uplifting side too. In François Ozon's film *Swimming Pool,* Charlotte Rampling says that literary prizes are like haemorrhoids: sooner or later every asshole gets one. In *Rerberg and Tarkovsky: The Reverse Side of 'Stalker',* this speech by Writer is taken as a vicarious monologue by Tarkovsky. Writer wanted to change 'them' but it's actually he who's been changed by 'them', has been gobbled up by 'them'. Tarkovsky's vision is uniquely, uncompromisingly his own—or so it seems to us. For his part, Tarkovsky believed that his 'entire life has consisted of compromises'. By now the camera has moseyed right up to Writer—this is his soliloquy, his Hamlet moment, his close-up. Or put it another way, whenever you want to pour your heart out Tarkovsky's camera is always there, moving subtly closer, ready to lend an ear and an eye. Writer's really distraught. The Zone is working its drippy magic as, sitting on the edge of the infinite drop, he peers into the depths of his own being, talking directly at us, encouraging a reciprocal response from this member of the audience.

So what kind of writer am I, reduced to writing a *summary* of a film? Especially since there are few things I hate more than when someone, in an attempt to persuade me to see a film, starts *summarizing* it, explaining the plot, thereby destroying any chance of my ever going to see it. In my defence I would say that *Stalker* is a film that can be summarized in about two sentences. So if summary means reducing to a synopsis, then this is the opposite of a summary; it's an amplification and expansion. This still begs the question of whether the composition of such a summary is a reasonable way to spend one's days. What is the purpose of such an exercise? The exercise is, of course, its own purpose, an end in itself. Whether it will amount to anything—whether it will add up to a worthwhile commentary, and whether this commentary might also become a work of art in its own right—is still unclear. The point is that, as a direct result of embarking on this summary, I am not in the despond in which Writer finds himself. I'm not perched on the edge of a tubular abyss in a soaking wet overcoat; I'm sitting at my desk in a nice warm cardigan. I'm getting on with something, making progress, moving towards a Room of my own. Certain kinds of writers, certain types of novelists, are reluctant to engage in anything that distracts them from their own work. Commentary, for them, is a distraction, of secondary or no importance. But there are other writers—and

I don't mean straight-down-the-line critics—for whom commentary is absolutely central to their own creative project, who insist that at some level commentary can turn out to be every bit as original as the primary work of the novelist. Besides, if mankind was put on earth to create works of art, then other people were put on earth to comment on those works, to say what they think of them. Not to judge objectively or critically assess these works but to articulate their feelings about them with as much precision as possible, without seeking to disguise the vagaries of their nature, their lapses of taste and the contingency of their own experiences, even if those feelings are of confusion, uncertainty or—in this case—undiminished wonder.

Writer has finished talking his talk and begins walking the walk towards the other two, through the sandy hummocks of the sand room. The camera angles slowly down to where he was standing, to where his feet were, to reveal something of significance that he left behind: a clue. We wait and look. But there's nothing. Just the sand, slightly disturbed but unconcerned.

Stalker is happy again. Deep down, Writer must be a really good man, if he made it through the meat grinder.

The meat grinder is a horrible place. Porcupine sent his brother to die there. His brother was a talented creature, a poet who wrote lines that Stalker proceeds to recite as if his life depends on it. Here's another quirk or feature of the Zone: it never happens that all three men are happy at once. Writer is really pissed now. He reckons Stalker cheated when they drew lots, is convinced that Stalker has chosen Professor as his favourite. Diddums! It's all getting a little fraught and fractious but here comes that black dog again, no longer looking like a messenger from the unconscious, just looking like a nice black doggy, padding through the puddles and all the bric-a-brac bobbing about in them as Writer harangues Stalker, telling him what a cheating little shit he is. They're in a room, backlit by a window with a view of the greenish world outside, tightly framed by an open doorway. The phone starts ringing. Writer keeps ranting, then picks it up furiously—No, this is not the clinic—before ranting on again. Then, abruptly, in another of those comic moments for which Tarkovsky is absolutely unrecognized, they look at the phone as the emperor of Brazil, Dom Pedro II, did when he first encountered the new invention: 'My God, it talks!' It's as if the whole film is a mysteriously extended version of one of those Orange Film Board–sponsored

'Don't let a phone ruin your movie' shorts.* This moment of unexpected comedy, as Robin Bird points out, has its origin in a documented quirk of history: soldiers scrambling through the destruction of Stalingrad would occasionally come across odd vestiges of civilization, 'such as ringing telephones.' Proceeding on the principle that if it talks it works, Professor ignores Stalker's warning—Don't touch!—picks it up (it looks a bit like one of those dynamite plungers in westerns) and dials. It's a rotary dial so this sequence has added fascination as gestural archaeology. In evolutionary terms the index finger enjoyed a long period of dominance in the era of the rotary phone but this action is now close to extinct. The index finger is entering a phase of quietude and disuse while the thumb enjoys a renaissance in the age of texting and mobiles. Professor gets through right away—and not to an automated answering system (which would have made the rotary dial a little problematic) but to an actual Russian-speaking human being. He's made a personal call, possibly long-distance, another reminder of the past, when phone calls were prohibitively expensive and one grabbed

---

* Scope, also, for an allusive YouTube-style redub: Professor answers the phone and says, 'Ah Michelangelo!'

every chance to make a call on someone else's dime. He has a coded conversation that does not make sense but is full of mutual threat, counterthreat and foreboding. I'm in the old building, he says, Bunker Four. (This is another accidental detail reinforcing—as always happens with stray coincidences in the realm of conspiracy theory—the idea of the film as prophecy of nuclear doom: it was reactor number four that went into gradual meltdown at Chernobyl.) Clearly Professor is intending to do *something,* though what that something might be—in the words of the Buffalo Springfield song—ain't exactly clear. The voice at the other end of the line—Russian, sinister-sounding—says that whatever it is he's plotting is revenge for the fact that he slept with Professor's wife twenty years ago. (Twenty years? That does seem a long time to have harboured a cuckold's grudge.) Voicing our unspoken questions, Writer asks Professor what he's planning. Imagine what it's like when everyone comes here, Professor explains. All the tin-pot dictators and would-be führers, people who come not for money but to change the world.* A good point, this. For many years

---

* Tarkovsky toyed with the idea of a 'subsequent film' in which Stalker himself develops some of these tendencies

now I have felt that I would like to be a dictator, the ruler of a regime that conforms in every detail to my ideas of how I think life should be lived and ordered. The world is full of people like me: idle Stalins and back-bedroom Lenins who are prevented from seizing and wielding power only by a chronic lack of drive, determination and ambition (desire backed by a willingness to achieve that which is desired). If we had access to the Room . . . I don't bring people like that, says Stalker. They're all standing in *a* room that for all we know might actually be *the* Room, in which case the Room would be a major disappointment, indistinguishable, in fact, from just about any other room. (Every bit as important as Tarkovsky's capacity for doubt is his *literalness;* how fantastic—I mean how *un*fantastic—to call their destination, this Holiest of Grails, the Room.) We're looking at them through the doorway still, the doorway without a door. Writer is fiddling with some string or twine and he's not impressed by Professor's little speech. No one cares enough about anything except their own trivial preoccupations. Revenge on your boss, something like that he can understand—strangely he doesn't

---

and 'starts forcibly to drag people to the Room and turns into a "votary", a "fascist". Bullying them into happiness.'

mention bigger sales or good reviews—but anything larger? No one who comes here is interested in that kind of stuff. A false distinction, surely. Dictators and ruthless autocrats start out with the idea of settling a few scores, want to advance to the next rung of the ladder so they can get even with whoever it was that snubbed them once, long ago, or for sleeping with their wife or some dimly remembered but unforgettable offence, if not the precise individual then the class or race of whom he is representative, and from there it's a very small leap to deciding that the whole lot of them must be exterminated, followed by any other class or group that looks like it might be capable of extermination or of revenging itself on you or your descendants, and before anyone knows quite how it happened all of Scotland bleeds and we have the Gulag system that stalks Tarkovsky's film like Banquo's ghost. Stalker says it's not possible to believe in happiness at the expense of someone else, which seems a little naive, especially to Writer, since the knowledge that someone might be a little unhappier than oneself—might have suffered worse reviews and even poorer sales—has been one of mankind's sources of solace, if not since the dawn of time, then certainly since the advent of literary journalism.

Writer pulls a switch and the lightbulb above his head, the bulb that looks like it's not good for anything except *not* working, surges into a light so bright that they all flinch from its glare. It's overexerted itself, though. After a few seconds, just like the light back home, when it was turned on by Stalker's missus, it goes out with a ping. The Zone might be fundamentally different from the world back there but defective wiring would seem to be a problem from which there is no escape. Buried beneath other, more overt layers of allegorical suggestiveness, could this be the very heart of the film? If their deepest wish, even if only negatively demonstrated, is for a decent power supply, then perhaps this constitutes a coded critique of the failure of communism as famously promised by Lenin: Soviet power plus electrification of the whole country.

TIME TO GET GOING. They step through the doorless doorway, the *way*. Writer, indulging in a last bit of baiting, tells Stalker he won't forgive him. As he does so we see what it is that he's been weaving together: a crown of thorns, no less. He puts it on and, credit where it's due, it fits him like a glove—but it's not a glove, of course, it's a crown of thorns. Ring any bells? Something biblical going on there? An allusion to Bob Dylan's 'Shelter from the Storm'? Writer as Christ? I dunno. Everything just is. Or isn't. But may be. So we'll have to leave it at that. Writer is wearing a crown of thorns of his own making but attempting to say exactly what this symbolizes or means is like making a rod for your own back. Quite an achievement, this, to have someone wearing a crown of thorns and to leave us the option of not buying into a theological or symbolic reading of something that seems to exist solely—it keeps you neither warm nor dry—in the realm of the symbolic. Tarkovsky's hostility to symbolic readings of his films extended to questions about the meaning of the Zone itself: 'I'm reduced to a state of fury and despair by such questions. The Zone doesn't symbolize anything, any more than anything else does in my films: the zone is the zone, it's life, and as he makes his way across it a man may break down or he may come through.' Ah, so the Zone *is* more than just a zone—it is, as Tarkovsky himself conceded, 'a test.'*

---

* As is the film itself. *Stalker* has long been synonymous both with cinema's claims to high art and a test of the viewer's ability to appreciate it as such. Anyone sharing Cate

Blanchett's enthusiasm—'every single frame of the film is burned into my retina'—attests not only to Tarkovsky's lofty purity of purpose but to their own capacity to survive at the challenging peaks of human achievement. So a certain amount of blowback is inevitable and desirable. Having given Tarkovsky short and rather grudging shrift in the various editions of his *Biographical Dictionary of Film*, David Thomson was moved, in 2008, to include *Stalker* (mentioned but not discussed in the *Dictionary*) in his pantheon of the thousand best movies, *'Have You Seen . . . ?'* But he remained dubious about the much-hyped Room at the heart of the Zone, suspecting that it would turn out to be 'an infinite, if dank enclosure in which an uncertain number of strangers are watching the works of Tarkovsky. Equally, it may be that as malfunction of one kind or another covers the world, we may have a hard time distinguishing the Room, the Zone, and the local multiplex.' This is infinitely preferable to the reverence that Tarkovsky tends to invite from his admirers—including himself. I have little instinct for personal reverence and, though I've not exactly been inundated with offers, I know I would hate to be revered myself. One of the things that I thought I would love as a writer, one of the perks of the job, would be having people come up to me to say how much they loved my books. And I do like it. For about ten seconds. After that I am desperate for the conversation to move on to any other topic. Actually, I need to slightly qualify what I just said about my own capacity for revering. I have a sizeable capacity for admiring people's *work* but I suspect that the verb 'to revere' describes a relation to people rather than things. Let's say I greatly admired *your* work and, at some point, had the chance to meet you. I would be overjoyed and would not be shy about expressing my admiration. But after a very short time, if I felt that you were interested in this as a basis for any kind of interaction, if you wanted to extend the reverence beyond what was considered politely necessary—if, in other words, you didn't get bored by being revered almost as quickly as I would be bored by revering—then I would start thinking you were a dick.

All of this is a lengthy way of introducing a pretty simple point: that if you have a considerable instinct for reverence and if you don't have an aversion to being revered, then it makes perfect sense to start revering yourself. If you're a public figure then this occurs in public. This, I think, is what happened to Tarkovsky.

Professor is distracted by the whining of the dog who sits on his haunches before the skeletal remains of two figures rotting in the dust, prior visitors—pilgrims or saboteurs?—who have perished for reasons that will never be revealed, which is not to say that they perished for no reason. The camera moves in on the perished pair: skeletons locked in a skeletal embrace.

THEY ARE IN a big, abandoned, derelict, dark damp room with what look like the remains of an enormous chemistry set floating in the puddle in the middle, as if the Zone resulted from an ill-conceived experiment that went horribly wrong. Off to the right, through a large hole in the wall, is a source of light that they all look towards. For a long while no one speaks. The air is full of the chirpy chirpy cheep cheep of birdsong. It's the opposite of those places where the sedge has withered from the lake and no birds sing. The birds are whistling and chirruping and singing like mad. Stalker tells Writer and Professor—tells *us*—that we are now at the very threshold of the Room. This is the most important moment in your life, he says. Your innermost wish will be made true here. And we believe him. This is the purpose of the journey, to make us believe the literal truth of what Stalker says at this point. Ideally, one would live one's whole life as though at this threshold; every moment would be like the one that is imminent. Not that you have to wish for anything explicitly, Stalker explains. You just have to concentrate on your past life. This makes the moment you enter the Room seem like death, when your life flashes before your eyes, when you look back on your life and assess its futility in the face of its absolute finitude and unrepeatability (or, if you are a Nietzschean, its eternal repeatability—repeatable but unvarying, which amounts to the same thing). Stalker grows reflective. When a man thinks of the past he becomes kinder, he says. A lovely idea, but manifestly untrue. There comes a point in your life when you realize that most of the significant experiences—aside from illness and death—lie in the past. To that extent the past is far more appealing than the future. The older you get the more time you spend thinking about the past, the things that have happened. Old people spend almost all of their time thinking about the past. But if their faces are anything to go by, this past fills them with bitterness as often as tenderness. The past becomes a source of regret; you think of hopes that were unrealized, disappointments, betrayals, failures, deceptions, all the things that

led to this point which could be so different, so much better, but which, however you reshuffle the deck, always
ends up at this point, leaves you holding—and lacking—
the same cards.

But the most important thing . . . Stalker is in a state of
more acute anxiety at this point than we have ever seen.
Or is he? It is as difficult to find the right word to describe
his expression—or expressions, plural, for his face seems
to be running the full gamut of emotions every fraction of
a second, or rather it is expressing a whole range of emotions simultaneously—as it is for him to say what is the
most important thing about this moment. It is a mixture
of exhaustion, turmoil, sincerity and hopelessness and . . .
His back is to the others. He walks away from them. The
most important thing is . . . to believe. To believe in this
moment, in the Room, is to bring its power into existence.
If you believe it will work it will work.

Stalker is talking about belief and one can see why, but,
strictly speaking, I think he means faith. The difference,
according to Alan Watts in *The Wisdom of Insecurity,* is
that 'the believer will open his mind to the truth on the
condition that it fits in with his preconceived ideas and
wishes. Faith, on the other hand, is an unreserved opening of the mind to the truth, whatever it may turn out

to be. Faith has no preconceptions; it is a plunge into the unknown. Belief clings, but faith lets go.' But then Miguel de Unamuno, in *Tragic Sense of Life,* says that faith 'is faith in hope; we believe what we hope for', as though faith and belief are one and the same. Or, again: 'Hope is the reward of faith. Only he who believes truly hopes; and only he who truly hopes believes. We only believe what we hope, and we only hope what we believe.' Hmm . . . Here we are, on the threshold of the Room, and these two back-of-the-alphabet thinkers have got us into a right old pickle about faith, hope and belief when we're meant to be concentrating on what we most want from life— which is definitely to not get distracted by a semantic squabble about faith, hope, belief and the extent to which they are or are not compatible with each other or with the desire for a lifetime's supply of free knapsacks.

Now you can go, says Stalker. Who wants to be first? Writer? It occurs to us, at this point, that it never crossed our minds that Professor and Writer really came to the Zone so that their deepest wishes could come true. In their different ways they were just curious. They wanted to see what the Zone was like, to see if it had the power to do what it claimed. Well, they're pretty convinced that it does. Which helps explain why Writer *doesn't* want to

go at all. Thinking of the past won't make him kinder.
Thinking of the past will make him think of bad reviews,
prizes that went to other people, acclaim that should have
been his, poor sales, not getting on three-for-two/front-
of-shop promotions, loss of inspiration—all the things
that he came to the frigging Zone to get shot of in the
first place. So, no thanks. Perfectly natural. Not many
people can confront the truth about themselves. If they
did they'd run a mile, would take an immediate and profound dislike to the person in whose skin they'd learned
to sit quite tolerably all these years. *Not* to have to face up
to the truth about oneself is probably high up on anyone's
actual—as opposed to imagined—wish list. Jung claimed
that 'people will do anything, no matter how absurd, in
order to avoid facing their own souls.' What could be
more absurd than to go to the Zone precisely for a rendezvous with one's own soul—and then, at the last moment,
decide against it? Except if evasion really is the name and
purpose of the game, then this kind of last-minute change
of heart is perfectly logical, a way of confirming, absolutely, that avoidance rather than revelation is the goal.
Besides, says Writer, putting down the crown of thorns,
don't you think it's humiliating, all this snivelling and
praying? This is a bit rich, given how he was snivelling

and whining back there on the edge of the tubular abyss. But he's right, of course, Stalker *is* pretty snivelling—but then who wouldn't be if they'd spent the day sleeping in wet puddles with only a soaking-wet coat as a blanket? What's wrong with praying? Stalker wants to know, not taking it personally. Well, for a start, it was developed—according to Nietzsche—to give stupid people something to do with their hands, to stop them fidgeting and making a nuisance of themselves in the quiet, sacred places of the earth. Never having got close to a condition of prayer—at school it seemed a question of holding your hands together and waiting for time to pass; in church, at funerals and weddings, it meant bowing your head and looking at your shoes and waiting for the whole thing to be over with so you could get stuck into the waiting flutes of champagne—I tend to agree. Bresson's Country Priest is forced to remind himself that 'the desire to pray is already prayer', but Stalker has no need of crumbled solace. His life is constant prayer, he's sort of praying even when he's not praying, when he's standing there with his brow getting more furrowed by the moment, having faith in what he hopes for and hoping for what he believes in or whatever. In the background, meanwhile, Professor is fiddling around, making something, maybe making a bigger and better crown of thorns than the one put together by Writer. Maybe that's his wish: to win the crown of thorns–making competition! I'm serious. We think we have huge goals in life but actually, when it comes to it, we'll settle quite happily for something trivial that we've had all the time and which made our lives bearable. I remember one of several conversations with my mum and dad about what they'd do if they won the football pools. The football pools: that, for many British people, was their equivalent of the Room, the thing that would make all their wishes come true. 'All I'd like to do,' my mum said with a mixture of pride and humbleness, 'is go down to the supermarket and buy the nicest piece of steak there. That's all I want.' 'You could do that NOW!' I yelled. What she really wanted was to forego the thing—*things,* actually, because she could probably have afforded to eat steak from the supermarket every day for the rest of her life—that she claimed she wanted. (In stark contrast to today's generation of consumers, who have no fear of getting into debt, my parents drummed into my head a very simple economy of expenditure: If you can't afford it, go without. Actually, that first part—'If you can't afford it'—was pretty superfluous since this was less about economics than an entire philosophy of 'going without'.) On one occasion when my wife and I took my parents out for dinner (an unusual event as they hated going to restaurants), we were surprised to see that my mum had actually eaten all of her steak. Then, when we got back home, we found that she had squirrelled half of it away and brought it home wrapped up in a napkin in her handbag. These meat-related sources of regret seem to run deep in my family. When my mother was in the early stage of what proved to be her terminal illness my father said that on occasions she *did* buy steak from the supermarket, always the cheapest cuts, and it was 'never very nice.' He also said that he had regrets about their diet of the last fifty years. He wished they 'had eaten more fat.' Not meat, *fat*. That would have been an excellent wish to have taken into the Room. Imagine: your deepest wish is that you had eaten more fat. This is to slightly misrepresent the Room, however, for Stalker never claims that the Room's powers are retrospective. You can go into the Room and eat all the fat you like *from now on* but you can't transform the life you have led into one in which, even during the lean years, you ate heaps of fat.

But perhaps that is and always will be one's deepest wish: to have the terms of the offer slightly amended so that it *can* be retrospectively applied, to build a time machine, to go back and have another go, another punt, another throw of the dice, this time knowing the result in advance. The question, I suppose, is this: is one's deepest desire always the same as one's greatest regret?

If so, then my greatest regret is, without doubt, one I share with the vast majority of middle-aged, heterosexual men: that I've never had a three-way, never had sex with two women at once. Is that pathetic or is it wisdom? If the former then it might well be the latter as well. I look back now and see that there were a couple of chances but, at the time—both times, in fact—it didn't occur to me. That's one of life's subtle lessons: you may never know when the opportunity to have the thing you most want will present itself—for the simple reason that, at that moment, it may not be the thing you most want. I remember very clearly when the first of these potential opportunities presented itself, in my squalid flat in Brixton in the mid-1980s: I wanted to get rid of Jane so that my girlfriend Cindy and I could have sex, even though I knew that Jane (with whom I had had sex on numerous occasions since we had officially broken up) and Cindy were not averse to this kind of thing. The sense of a wasted chance was further exacerbated by the fact that, years later, when I had broken up with Cindy, she did in fact have sex with Jane and an unidentified third party (male). The other occasion was in Brighton when my girlfriend from Belgrade was visiting and we went to a party where we all took ecstasy and my friend Kathy told me that she and my girlfriend from Belgrade were going to have a lesbian affair, which was fine with me as long as I could be around too. The problem was that Kathy's boyfriend, Michael, was also around (and likewise wished I wasn't).

You think this is unworthy of the moment and the mystical opportunity of the Room? Well, that's for the Room to decide. The Room reveals all: what you get is not what you *think* you wish for but what you most *deeply* wish for. In which case my fear is that my deepest wish might not be to have had Jane sitting on my face and Cindy on my dick but something really embarrassing, something that I would not want to be made public. Like what? That instead of basking in the fact that I'd managed to get a squalid, rent-controlled flat in Brixton I'd somehow cobbled together money for the deposit to buy a flat in the area when prices, as a result of the riots—or 'uprisings' as we insisted on calling them—were at an all-time low, ideally a council flat during the big Thatcherite

sell-off to which we were all bitterly opposed. I bet that's
the universal wish of most people in the Western world:
that they'd got on the property ladder earlier. Even the
ones who got on the property ladder early, who realized
there was no point supporting Scargill and the miners,
who bought flats while the rest of us were sticking 'Coal
not Dole' badges on our donkey jackets, probably wish
they'd got on the property ladder earlier, before council flats were up for grabs, or, failing that, the moment
they went on sale, when you could buy a hard-to-let
for a thousand quid and still have change left over for
the first issue of cut-price British Telecom shares. What
else? I keep coming back to the 1980s, when I could have
grown my hair long, before it became all grey and tragic,
before I began looking like the kind of middle-aged man
constantly thinking of all the three-ways—two at any
rate—that he didn't have, that went begging, like three-
bedroom council flats that are now worth three hundred
times what they were thirty years ago.

But let's assume the Room's power is effective immediately, not retroactively. If your deepest desire is the
one manifested by your daily life and habits, then mine,
apparently, is to potter about, to potter my life away, drift-

ing from desk to kitchen (to make tea), from house to café (to have coffee). It all comes down to that line in *Solaris* about never knowing when we're going to die. If I had a week left to live it would be absurd to potter around my house like this. I'd rather be doing something exciting (though what that something might be for the moment escapes me). No, I need to give this a bit of thought. If I had a week left to live? Fly to an idyllic beach in Thailand or the Bahamas? But then I'd spend twelve hours on a plane and another three days shattered by jet lag, lying awake in the middle of the night, too tired to get up, and flopping around in the day, trying to stay awake so that I could sleep the next night. So it's difficult. The basic assumption is that if you had very little time left you would not do what you're doing now. But that's why this life of the writer, this life where you spend your time doing pretty much what you want, is quite different. So, given that I probably am going to be around for a while, this is pretty much my deepest desire at the moment, to sit here scribbling, trying to fathom out what my deepest desire might be.

In any case the whole idea of the Room is a joke. Perhaps our deepest wish in life is that there could be a place like this, a Room where our deepest wish comes true. Extrapolating from that, we don't want to get to the point where we discover that we actually don't want this Room to exist, that even if it existed we wouldn't enter it, that even if we could buy ourselves the nicest piece of steak in the supermarket we would save the money instead or spend it on beer and crisps, that even if I did get the chance for a three-way it would turn out that I couldn't get it up because I felt the odd man out, that it was actually a two-way with a third person (me) feeling superfluous. We want the Room to be external to ourselves, like the football pools or the lottery. We want *it* to do the work, want it to be a window on to another world, not a mirror reflecting back to ourselves the inadequate or shameful nature of our own desires, which probably do not operate on this one vote, once, kind of basis. One's deepest desire changes from day to day, moment to moment. There were plenty of occasions, in my twenties, when my most intense desire—so intense that it was impossible to see beyond it—was to have a beer, to get to the boozer before last orders, before time was called. Those days are gone but there are still times—when I'm in the cinema, watching a film I've wanted to see for ages—when all I want to do, the thing that I crave with every fibre of my being, is to shut my eyes and take a nap. ('The eye wants to sleep,' writes the poet, 'but the head is no mattress.')

Anyway, the long and the short of it is that Writer doesn't want to go into the Room or, in Stalker's optimistic reading of the situation, is not ready to go in just yet. This reluctance or hesitation is a specifically middle-aged problem. In your twenties there'd be no disjuncture at all between what you thought you wanted and your innermost wish; both would be the same, lying at the same depths within. It's one of the reasons why middle-aged people are reluctant to take powerful psychedelic drugs. I had the idea that in my mid-fifties I would start taking LSD again, was actually looking forward to seeing that acid ripple of the ground again, but now that it's only a few years away, the prospect seems altogether less appealing than it did a decade ago. What kind of stuff would tripping unearth? Probably that I had no desire to trip. Even if I waited for a perfect day, for cloudless weather in the sky and in the head, it might turn out that, unbeknownst to me, a dreadful storm was about to brew up in the head, in which case the bright conditions outside would only exacerbate the abysmal depression within, that before I knew it I'd end up in the damp and clammy meat grinder, putting one foot in front of another in a state of abject terror.

How about Professor, then? Yep, he's up for it. Well, this is a surprise, especially since he's got his knapsack back. A while back he was all for calling it a day but now he's ready to take the plunge. Good man. He goes to get whatever it is he's been fiddling with but it's definitely not a crown of thorns. It looks like an absolutely state-of-the-art thermos, far better than the one he's been lugging around, capable of keeping drinks piping hot or icy cold for thousands of years. What could it be? A soul-ometer, quips Writer, but then Professor drops an absolute bombshell: it's not a thermos flask, it's a bomb. What the . . . ? Yes, a twenty-kiloton *bomb*. He's a secular jihadist, a militant proto-Dawkinsite, declaring war on the believers, on those who have faith in the transformative power of the Room. Professor insists that he's not a maniac but, at this moment, he looks and sounds exactly like an elderly nutter with a bomb. He and his colleagues back at the Institute decided to destroy the Room in case it got into the wrong hands, to stop people coming here whose deepest wish was to control mankind and enslave the world, the lazy Hitlers and couch Stalins. But then some of his conspirators at the Institute had a change of heart. They decided that even if it was a miracle it was still part of nature.*

---

* Reading about and around *Stalker* or Tarkovsky, one cannot go for long without this word *miracle* cropping up. 'My discovery of Tarkovsky's first film was like a miracle,' said Bergman. He was talking about *Ivan's Childhood,* but continued in a way that could not but put one in mind of *Stalker,* as if his innermost cinematic wishes had come true. 'Suddenly, I found myself standing at the door of a room, the keys of which had, until then, never been given to me. It was a room I had always wanted to enter and where he was moving freely and fully at ease.' Kris, near the end of *Solaris,* also seems to be looking ahead to what the director might come up with next: 'The only thing that remains for me is to wait. For what? I don't know. A new miracle?' There were more miracles to come from Tarkovsky—though none of these took the form of further employment for Donatas Banionis, who played the part of Kris. The caption at the beginning of *Stalker* describes the Zone as 'a miracle.' A still from *The Sacrifice* in the updated edition of *Sculpting in Time* was summarized by Tarkovsky with these words: ' "Little Man" waters the tree his father planted, patiently awaiting the miracle which is no more

than the truth.' And the miraculous, it seems, was not confined to the effects created on-screen, but was part of the process by which they were achieved. Looking back on the numerous obstacles that had to be overcome with so many of the shots and set ups, production designer Rashit Safiullin said, 'Every time it was a little miracle-making.'

The prevalence of miracles and the routinely miraculous in Tarkovsky perhaps hints at something more general about the society and history of which he was a product. One of the goals of Marxism-Leninism or of historical materialism is to do away with the category of the miraculous—in history, as in logic, there are no surprises. As the promise of the Soviet Revolution hardened into the relentless bureaucracy of Stalinism, so the opposite occurred. The thoroughness with which everyone was caught in the mechanism of the totalitarian system meant that any escape or exemption acquired the quality of a miracle. 'The greater the degree of centralisation,' writes Nadezhda Mandelstam in *Hope Against Hope,* 'the more impressive the miracle.' The more intolerable life became the more it became 'impossible' to live without miracles. Addressing letters to Stalin in the hope of clemency or of having a sentence commuted—'what is such a letter but a plea for a

Quite so. Everything we see in the Zone is conceivably just a part of nature. What seems a miracle is the ground rippling due to some geomorphologic activity that one cannot understand. The disappearing bird is a fluke of the light. The sudden gust of wind, blowing in from nowhere in the midst of a calm day, is a freak gust of wind. Anyway, some of Professor's friends decided

---

miracle?'—meant that people lived in the routine expectation of miracles: 'They had become part of our life.' On the occasions that these pleas were answered—as happened to Osip Mandelstam in 1934—people were 'overjoyed.' But, Nadezhda continues in terms curiously appropriate to *Stalker,* 'one must remember that even if they got their miracles, the writers of such letters were doomed to bitter disappointment. This they were never prepared for, despite the warning of popular wisdom that miracles are never more than a flash in the pan, with no lasting effect. What are people left with in the fairy tales after their three wishes have come true? What becomes, in the morning, of the gold obtained in the night from the lame man? It turns into a slab of clay or a handful of dust. The only good life is one in which there is no need for miracles.'

against blowing up the Zone, but that's exactly what he's here to do. Exactly in the sense of probably. He came here with the idea that his innermost wish was to blow up the Zone, to get in and slam the door behind him; to make sure that he was the last to avail himself of its promised magic. But even at this late stage there's scope for doubt, even now that he's made up his mind it's possible his innermost wish won't let him do what he's determined he must do. This is one of the lessons of the Zone: sometimes a man doesn't want to do what a man thinks he wants to do. Besides, there's no guarantee that the physical destruction of the Room will diminish belief in its power. On the contrary, obliteration might generate more stories about it and heighten the mythical status of the place where it *used to be* until it is brought into re-existence on the site—and by virtue—of its own absence.

Stalker wanders off to consider what, from his point of view, both as a devotee of the Zone and as someone who earns his living from it, can only be very bad news. Then he spins round and tries to snatch the bomb from the Professor. They have an old-bloke scuffle, like an outtake from *Bumfights,* but then Writer wades in and—three times—chucks Stalker back into the murky water with

all the lightbulbs and stuff from the chemistry set floating in it. Strangely, Professor objects to this intervention,
even as Stalker comes back yet again, only to be flung into
the foreground. Impossible, at this point, not to think of
the bit near the end of Don DeLillo's *White Noise,* when
Willie Mink gives a deranged lecture on room behaviour: 'The point of rooms is that they're inside. No one
should go into a room unless he understands this. People
behave one way in rooms, another way in streets, parks
and airports. To enter a room is to agree to a certain kind
of behaviour. It follows that this would be the kind of
behaviour that takes place in rooms.'

Which raises the question of whether, on the threshold of a room that is not just any room but *the* Room,
all this talk of blowing the place to kingdom come, all
this brawling and scuffling and throwing each other into
puddles, is entirely appropriate.

Stalker would be the one to know but he's had all the
fight knocked out of him. He picks himself up again,
wants to know why Professor wants to destroy people's
hope. This place that is all that's left to them on earth,
the only place they can come to. Why destroy their hope?
The awfulness of what is about to be done revives Stalker
sufficiently to make him rush Professor again—only to

get thrown to the ground by Writer, who has grown increasingly angry. (Professor looks like he's about to have a heart attack—the scuffling has knocked the puff out of him too.) Writer launches into a diatribe against Stalker. He's a louse, enjoying the power of God almighty. No wonder he never enters the Room—he's got everything he wants, all the power and mystery. Stalker has rarely looked happy; he has always appeared burdened by the job of being a Stalker, now—with his face bloodied and bruised, his eyes red with tears—he looks utterly dejected. And he's literally snivelling whereas before he was just acting in a snivelling sort of way. Stalkers are not allowed to enter the Room, he snivels. They can't even enter the Zone with any ulterior motive. But yes, you're right, he tells Writer. I'm a louse, I've never done any good in this life, I've never even given anything to my wife. I don't have any friends. But don't take everything from me. Everything has been taken from me, on the other side of the barbed wire, he says. All that's mine is here, in the Zone. My happiness, my freedom, my self-respect. I bring people here, people like me—the desperate, the tormented. They have nothing else to hope for. And I bring them here. Only I, the louse, can help them.

Having got so much off their chests everyone simmers

down. Writer is having doubts himself. Why did Porcupine hang himself? Because he came here with mercenary motives. So why didn't he come back to repent? Because, he understands now, not all wishes will be granted here, only your innermost wish, which, in Porcupine's case, was for money. Confronted by his true nature, he hanged himself. The truth revealed by the Room is ontological. 'Each one of us comes into the world with her or his unique possibility—which is like an aim, or, if you wish, almost like a law,' says a character in John Berger and Nella Bielski's play *A Question of Geography*. 'The job of our lives is to become—day by day, year by year, more conscious of this aim so that it can at last be realized.' Unless you're a paedophile, say, or any one of a dozen other types of sicko. Then the job of your life is to bury that urge, to make sure you never get near the gates of a primary school or anything that might turn out to be the Room.

Another, less dramatic, scenario: what if you got here and went into the Room, believing in it absolutely, and it turned out that you didn't have an innermost wish, that all the things you thought you wished for you didn't actually want? You leave the Room, leave the Zone and, unlike Porcupine, nothing happens. Jack shit. Would you conclude from this that you were absolutely content, purring on a daily basis like a cat or a dog whose bowl of milk was constantly replenished? Unlikely. Or at least if you *had* been content—without realizing it—now you would most certainly be filled with discontent. You would conclude that the Room did not work. That you'd been sold a pup. That Stalker had not undergone the changes that he went through as Tarkovsky and the much-put-upon Strugatskys reworked, rewrote and reshot the film. You would phone him, demand a refund, threaten to blacken his name, turn him in to the authorities or, at the very least, refuse to recommend him to friends considering a once-in-a-lifetime trip to the much-vaunted Zone. Of course Stalker would have none of it. In the extremely unlikely event that he returned or even answered your calls he would insist that it *had* worked, that it was working perfectly. And so you would be left seething, dissatisfied, cheated, unable to accept that this was your innermost wish, your innermost nature.

They are all back where they were before Professor unveiled his bomb, his stainless steel IED, before the scuffle in this waterlogged place, on the threshold of the Room, whose light can be seen, off to the right. Stalker is on his knees, collapsed on the floor. Writer is holding forth like a detective who has just solved a difficult case, who has spotted the clues and unravelled the contradictions that escaped the attention of other, less subtle, minds. And he's not finished. How do we know it's true, that the Zone grants all your wishes? Who actually said that the Room granted these wishes? One assumes Writer is speaking to Stalker but Professor replies, *He* did, meaning Stalker, as if the whole idea of the Zone and the Room were entirely his invention.*

Writer is at the edge of the Room and, overcome by his own oratorical prowess, stumbles forward, is about to *fall* into the Room, is about to tumble into having his own innermost wish accidentally realized—more sales than Wilbur Smith, more critical acclaim than Sebald, more chicks than Bukowski—but Stalker pulls him back and they huddle on the ground together. The phone is

---

* A view occasionally endorsed by Tarkovsky, in a 1981 interview, for example: 'I completely agree with the suggestion that it was Stalker who had created the Zone's world in order to invent some sort of faith, a faith in that world's existence.' And again, in 1986: 'The Zone doesn't exist. It's Stalker himself who invented his Zone.'

ringing again. Writer puts his arm around Stalker's shoulders. Professor stands up, begins dismantling his thermos-bomb, chucking bits of it into the water, asking the question that is on everyone's lips—What is the point in coming here?

The purpose of coming here was to get to the point where that question could be asked of oneself rather than someone else. There always comes a moment in the writing of a book when its purpose is revealed: the moment when the urge—Nabokov's famous 'throb'—that led one to consider writing it is made plain. Actually there are two moments, or, if it makes sense to put it like this, the moment comes in two phases. First when one realizes that yes, there *is* a book here—however faintly it can be discerned—not just a haphazard collection of jottings and crossings-out clustered round an inadequately formed idea. Since, in principle, getting to that point should be easy, it's disheartening to find that so much time and energy have to be wasted, that so many pointless detours, irritating obstacles, self-imposed tests and excuses (that voice constantly whispering or crying out 'Stop!') conspire to get in the way. But at the point when you realize that there *is* a book, even a short one with little hope of critical approval or large sales, you see that all those diversions were necessary and inevitable and so, strictly speaking, were not diversions at all (even if the whole journey is, ultimately, no more than a diversion). From that point on—the point that Kafka said must be reached—there is no turning back and, despite setbacks, the going gets generally easier. The next moment comes not when the book is finished—that is better conceived as the last bit of the previous phase—but some time after it is published, when you see it for what it is (weirdly, page proofs always retain some of the glow of how it was intended to be rather than what it is). Then you see that actually those big desires and hopes, your deepest wishes, turned out not to be so deep at all, that actually even to consider life and writing in terms of a single wish is absurd, that there are numerous wishes and numerous books to be written—or, by reference to something mentioned earlier, further extensions (more *rooms*) to be built, more beer to be drunk, and more countries to be napalmed. You wonder if you wouldn't have been better off summarizing a different film, *Where Eagles Dare,* say, or writing a different book, about tennis perhaps. There's no Room, or at least this one, this room, wasn't it. And so one sets off again, trying to find another.

Since we've come this far, since we are still on the threshold of the Room and could conceivably sneak in there while these three are recovering from all that scuffling, perhaps I should say what it is that I most want from—what is my deepest wish for—this book. Easy: success. Success that, by definition, will be *enormous* success. If it is published, if someone will deign to publish this summary of a film that relatively few people have seen, then that will constitute a success far greater than anything John Grisham could ever have dreamed of. And that wish, as you can tell, has been granted. As a result the original wish has been updated and upgraded because I'm now thinking that this summary that is the opposite of a summary does have some commercial appeal—in an admittedly niche sort of way—and is actually deserving of serious critical attention, maybe even a little prize of some kind.

Professor tosses bits of the bomb into one part of the waterlogged room, other bits into other parts. There are lots of bits—it's more complicated, bomb-wise, than it looked at first—but there's a lot of water too. It's not only the wiring, the plumbing is shot to hell too. The phone is no longer ringing. There is the sound of birds again and of dripping water, the two not entirely distinct, as if the birds were amphibious, still partly fish, the sounds one might have heard in the early days of creation, before there were people, when there was no one around to hear, when there was no difference between god and evolution, and Darwin himself was probably just a swimming fish, trying to breathe with wings or fly with gills. The three of them sit there and the camera pulls back, into the Room itself, revealing the water-immersed tiled floor. (None of the humans has made it into the Room—only the camera whose deepest wish has been realized before our eyes.) They're worn out, by the journey, by the scuffle, by the combination of disappointment and enlightenment, by the uncertain distinctions between faith, hope and belief, by the complex simplicity of whatever it is they have learned or not learned, by not knowing whether the lessons of evolution—of learning as you go—are ever going to be over with. The light, which has been silvery and dank, glows gradually golden and warm, then fades, Turrell-ishly, to dank and silver again. Stalker says what he said at the beginning: How quiet it is here. Can you feel it? It isn't, but we can. He wonders why he doesn't come and live here with his wife and child, Monkey, where there's no one else, where no one can harm them. Is it because at some level he doesn't want to? That maybe the Zone won't live up to his hopes after all, will be unable to sustain, as Fitzgerald said of Gatsby (we are back there again), the colossal vitality of his illusions? A crack of thunder, of unseen lightning. Bringing rain: internal rain, rain that knows how to behave in a room. A shower of room rain, gentle at first, falling between us and the three men sitting there. Then becoming heavier and louder, more storm than shower, falling into the flooded area between us and them. As much a shower of light as of rain even though the rain has no wish to be anything other than what it is. Any such desire evaporated long ago but it will come around again as surely as day follows night. As the rain rains Professor chucks more parts of his bomb—harmless now—into the water which is a thousand small explosions of glitter. The storm is soon a shower again—light rain, raining light—and then the shower is over except for the usual drip and drop and they continue sitting there. Professor lobs the last bits of his bomb into the glitter-ripple of water. Drip, drip. We can see part of it, parts of the bomb that is no longer a bomb, resting on the tiles beneath the water, gone the way of the machine gun and syringes—the opposite of souvenirs—seen earlier.

'Everything, after passing through time, returns to

eternity,' writes Unamuno. 'The scenes of life pass before us as in a film, but on the other side of time the film is one and indivisible.' A couple of curious fish nuzzle up to the ex-bomb, ascertaining whether or not it might be edible. A black film, inky, with threads of blood—from the fish?—spreads over the water as the sound builds of a train moving swiftly and blaring a bit of Ravel's *Boléro,* a piece of music whose place in film history is indelibly linked with Bo Derek and Dudley Moore in *10.* Not that Bo Derek is on anyone's mind, certainly not the fishes', as vibrations from the train make the water rock and sway over the harmless remains of the bomb and the curiously harmless fish, causing the black oily film to sway and shudder over bomb, fish, water and screen.

IT SEEMS LIKE THE END but it's not the end. We are back at the bar, *in* the bar in fact, looking out through the smeary door that has not been washed in the how-ever-long-it-is interlude while they have been busy not thinking about Bo Derek, having the time of their lives— though not quite the time they thought they were going to have—in the Zone. The bar door is open. Across the stretch of industrial water we can see the power station, looking all Didcot and grey because—oh yes, we're also back in black-and-white, here in the world that is not the Zone. The noise of the train, the 6:10 to Boléro. Just outside the door is Stalker's wife, all bundled up in a sheepskin coat and she has their daughter, Monkey, with her, and some crutches leaning by the stairs. The wife comes up the stairs to the boozers—there they are, the three of them. Luger, the barman of few words, is there too, and he's the first to see her. Uh-oh. They're back, though we have no idea how they got back. Stalker kept telling them there was no going back but, among the lessons learned and not learned, one might be that there is nothing *but* going back.*

---

* This would certainly seem to be the lesson of *The Return* and *The Banishment* by Andrei Zvyagintsev. *The Return* (2003) starts spectacularly with a group of boys jumping from a high watchtower into deep water. Ivan, the youngest of a pair of brothers, is scared of making the jump so his brother, Andrei, and the others leave him up there, shivering and ashamed. The next day they learn from their mother that their father has returned after an

absence of twelve years. Played by Konstanin Lavronenko (who looks like Russia's answer to George Clooney *and* José Mourinho), he's evidently some kind of gangster. The three of them, father and two sons, go on a road trip but it's more like a pirated Russian offshoot of the Duke of Edinburgh's Award scheme than a vacation. The father is a stern taskmaster; he has the unyielding harshness of a man who has done time and learned how to survive in the brutal world of the Russian prison system. He bullies and scares them and it all starts to seem like a test of the boys' manly mettle. The buried loot or hidden treasure or whatever it is the father is trying to retrieve leads, after numerous setbacks, tests and diversions to a remote island—the father makes the boys row there after the boat's engine gives out—dominated by another rickety old watchtower. Vanya climbs the tower, the hated father climbs after him, falls and dies. As a result of the skills the father has taught them in the course of their trip the boys are able to travel back home, without the father's body, which sinks with the boat on the crossing back from the island.

The Return cries out to be interpreted as a return to— and extension of—the Zone, to the kind of cinematic space or vision discovered by Tarkovsky. (Even the walls of the abandoned building where the boys play and fight in the opening scenes seem Zonal; on the island there is a verdant meadow, in the middle of which stands an abandoned hut.) Tarkovsky bequeathed his progeny a sense of the visionary potential of film, of space. But he is a hard and gruelling taskmaster. If you want to follow his example you have also to kill him off. Once that has occurred you can make your own way into new, uncharted cinematic wilderness. I apologize for this explanation—one part Harold Bloom and one part ill-digested psychoanalysis—but you take the point.

The problem—though this becomes fully evident only with Zvyagintsev's next film—is that he has *not* killed off the father, has not shaken off the huge and inhibiting debt to the master. Or perhaps, having killed him off in *The Return,* Zvyagintsev devotes the whole of *The Banishment* (2007) to atoning for this crime. Three of the first half dozen shots evoke, in turn, *Nostalghia* (car driving through landscape, curving out of and then back into shot), *Stalker* (bleak industrial zone, freight train) and *Solaris* (car hurtling into urban abyss). Thereafter it's impossible not to succumb to spotting Tarkovsky allusions and references: kids leafing through books, or gazing at an orange fire (albeit in a hearth); Bach; Leonardo (in the form of a jigsaw puzzle of *The Annunciation* being completed by children). So overt is the Tarkovsky bequest that, at one point, when the wife and mother, Vera, takes a sip of her drink and puts the glass on the table one half expects her to start moving it telekinetically. She is pregnant but the child is not her husband's (Lavronenko again, back from the dead or, if you prefer, returned from *The Return*); it—i.e., the film—is Tarkovsky's. The house where all this occurs is located in a barren and beautiful landscape that, like the altogether more fecund setting of *Mirror,* is replete with childhood memories. 'Why isn't the creek flowing?' asks Kir, the little boy, of his father, Lavronenko. *Because,* I found myself silently responding, *Uncle Andrei has used it all up.* 'Did you see it [*i.e., Uncle Andrei's*] flow [*of images*]?' asks Kir again. 'I saw nothing else,' says Lavronenko, taking the words out of my mouth. By the end, needless to say, the rains replenish the creek, which starts to flow, turning it into a Zoney stream, complete with everyday detritus hallowed by the fact of being filmed. There is more to *The Banishment* than its Tarkovsky infatuation. Doubtless, I am guilty of the crime of which I am accusing Zvyagintsev: being so absorbed by *Stalker* that I can see nothing but Tarkovsky, so steeped in his view of the world that I mistake it for the world itself. Certainly Tarkovsky is not the only director whose work is, as they say, cited or sighted but he is the dominant force and I can think of no other film so dominated—to the point almost of self-immolation—by the work of another director.

The end of *The Banishment* echoes the beginning with a shot of an almond tree and a car winding its way along the road that runs beside it. Except this is not quite the same as the beginning, for the camera then tracks to the side to some peasant women—who seem to have stepped out of a Brueghel painting (which carries with it the tacit suggestion that they have also stepped out of a Tarkovsky film, at one remove). Suddenly we're in a different film. It's as if, playing alongside the movie we've just seen, was another, which we now have the option of watching.

This artful if rather distracting sideways shift into another movie alerted me to something that I had, as it

The wife could be forgiven for thinking that they've been here all the time, on a colossal bender, or having ingested a powerful psychedelic, getting so fucked up that mere survival—the avoidance of liver failure or mental breakdown—seems like an achievement. They all look pretty messed up: rumpled, mud-smeared, damp, but not totally Boris-Mikhailoved—nothing that couldn't have been the result of a half-decent drinking session. If she didn't know her husband better . . . Well, whatever it is they've been up to they're none the wiser for it. Or per-

---

were, known but not realized about Tarkovsky. Like all the greatest filmmakers he immerses you so completely in his world that it never occurs to you—unless it is by design, à la Godard at the end of *Le Mépris* (a deliberate limiting that serves also as a deeper immersion)—that the world on-screen ceases to exist at the edges of screen. The best directors all invert Coriolanus's claim that there is a world elsewhere. No, the world beyond the screen is just a continuation of the world we are seeing. To either side and behind there is more of the same. We are not even in a cinema; we are in a world. Or, rather, there is nothing but cinema; there is only the Zone.

haps they're a hell of a lot wiser if, by wiser, we mean sadder and if, by sadder, we mean damper. The thing about wisdom is that it rarely reveals itself in appearances; one never knows what it looks like in human form.

But wait—something *is* different. They've got a dog with them. The dog, from our point of view, is the only proof that they've been where they say, proof that this place called the Zone exists. It's like the rose that Coleridge mentions, the one you dreamed you found in paradise (the one, to be honest, that I've had cause to mention elsewhere, in a not unrelated context) and then, on waking, find in your bed. Stalker is feeding the dog. Other than that nothing has changed, but then that's always the way when you go anywhere and come back. Nothing has ever changed, even if the place you come back to has changed unrecognizably, which is definitely not the case with this dump. The lonesome whistle is still blowing, doesn't sound any less lonesome. Luger is still smoking and the bar is still a bit of a dump. The flickering light, it goes without saying, is still flickering. The wife comes into the bar, one part local sheriff confronting three gunslingers, one part stern mum whose adolescent son and his mates have been caught drinking. And they *have* been drinking, we can see now: they've got a beer each and who can blame them? No one could begrudge them a few beers after what they've been through, even if it's not clear what it is they've been through. She asks about the dog and plonks herself down on the bench. Does either of you two want dogs? They don't. Writer has five at home already—seems a lot but maybe he's got a bigger house than we imagined. So you love dogs, do you, she says. That's a good thing (as though liking dogs could ever be anything other than a good thing).*

---

* If she'd asked me I'd have said yes in an instant. I'd love to have a dog. Or would I? The fact that my wife and I have not got a dog despite thinking about getting a dog, mulling it over and talking about nothing else for five years, suggests that maybe we don't want a dog. In some way, though, *this* dog—a dog that looks more like a concentrated idea of dog than any particular breed of dog—is there to remind me that I do want a dog, that it's not for nothing that we spend all our time talking about getting a dog and looking at dog websites and that we already have a name for the dog that we've not got around to getting: Monkey, named after Stalker's daughter, even though

So, says the wife, are we going?

The dog trots out of the bar, followed by Stalker and his wife. (Could it be that Stalker did set foot in the Room after all, that his deepest wish was to have a dog?) Writer and Professor—the pair of them look so dirty they could be in a socialist-realist drama about coal miners—watch them go: Stalker, his wife, the dog, and Monkey, their kid. Writer is smoking a cigarette, squinting through the smoke in a writerly way, watching them go, looking like he's learnt something, something that he may one day put

---

this is a potentially confusing name for a dog, just as Cat or Fish would be. But then—this is why we go round in circles the whole time—we also know that the reason we have not got a dog yet is because there is only one dog we want, Dotty, our friends' lurcher. That would be my deepest wish: for our friends suddenly to say, 'You've been such good friends to us over the years that we've decided to give you Dotty, even though a lurcher needs lots of open space and you don't even have a garden and she will miss us and the Kent countryside so badly that she'll probably just pine away and die in a fortnight.'

into writing: *An empty bar, possibly not even open, with a single table . . .*

From here on we are in a realm of loveliness unmatched anywhere else in cinema. We are able to believe in something blatantly untrue, an amendment to the idea that men were put on earth to create works of art: that the cinema was invented so that Tarkovsky could make *Stalker,* that our greatest debt to the Lumière brothers is that they enabled this film to be made.

SWITCH TO COLOUR, to the daughter, Monkey, in profile and in close-up, swathed in a golden-brown head scarf, walking through the bare blur of trees, with the dog. So, colour is not the unique preserve of the Zone after all. Something that is almost snow—sleet, gobs of rain, sky-blossom—is falling. The music on the sound track is that spooky electronic drone again that we heard right at the beginning, before they went to the Zone. We can still see only her head bobbing along but the focus is not as tight and we watch her moving through more of the landscape, covered in snow or pale ash. The lake or river is a dull grey. As the camera pulls back we see that Monkey is not walking; she is on her father's shoulders, and the landscape, though desolate, has a desolate beauty. They make their way through the wasteland, Stalker, his wife and child, Monkey, and the dog. In Kenzaburo Oë's story, 'The Guide (*Stalker*),' a dinner guest, Mr. Shigeto, comments on 'the excellent acting of the dog in [this] scene'. Mr. Shigeto's wife disagrees: 'Fine acting on the part of dogs is mere coincidence, with the exception of super movie dogs like Lassie or Rin Tin Tin. And even their acting, she claimed, wasn't acting in the truest sense, for their roles were always the same.' She is here echoing a point made by Béla Balázs, that only 'plants and animals do not act for the director.' If they are right then this actually fits in well with what Tarkovsky required of his human actors too. Donatas Banionis—Kris in *Solaris*—was uneasy with the director's lack of interest in psychological motivation and his exacting demands that the characters move a certain number of steps or remain quite still for a precise number of seconds. For Banionis this was not acting but 'posing' or 'counting one-two-three.' Dogs can't count but this one does everything required of him, moving like the director's counter on a Ludo board, tail wagging, tagging along with Stalker and his wife and child.* One assumes that if the dog had strayed into the Room he would have wanted to go on as he was, with his untroubled doggy life. Or maybe not. Maybe he was lonely padding around the Zone, wandered into a room and, although he didn't know this room was *the* Room, his innermost wish—to be adopted and taken home by a nice family of humans—was granted. (Inconceivably cynical, surely, to suggest that his deepest wish was to be a movie-star dog?)

Paradise Lost ends with Adam and Eve making their way out of Eden 'with wandering steps and slow.' There is something similarly touching about this scene, though now it is a nice little family (with a new dog) and it's not a life of exile and unprecedented adventure that lies ahead but a return to the familiar contentments and frustrations of home. It's reminiscent, in its dreary, postindustrial way, of the pure winter scenes—enhanced by the Brueghel echoes—in *Mirror*. In the background, across the lake

---

* Looking back on the sequence when Stalker is lying in water and the dog comes up to him, director of photography Knyazhinsky remarks fondly that this 'fantastic dog', who only understood commands in Estonian, 'literally worked miracles': a real Zone dog!

or the river, is the power station, pouring out clouds of smoke or steam. The dog pads on ahead, tail wagging, and then circles back to join the others. They look like the last family on earth, sole survivors of the catastrophe that everyone else calls life.

A HAND POURS white milk, the sweet milk of interspecies concord, from a triangular carton (a precursor of the Tetra Pak) into a wooden bowl, careless about the spillage but conscious, surely, that something has spilled over from a similar sequence in *Mirror*. The dog laps it up like a cat. It's one of the best bits of lapping up in the history of cinema. No one has ever lapped up milk like this before or since—another excellent bit of lap-acting on the part of the dog who was unaware he was acting or, by the standard of the Method, had achieved a state of such complete immersion in his character that he was acting out of—in the sense of *in*—his skin. Stalker lies down by the bowl while the dog continues lapping up the milk like there's no tomorrow. Stalker is back home and, once again, we're back where we started. You can't imagine how tired I am, Stalker tells his wife, stretched out horizontally on the floor of a room crammed with books. He's got more books than an Oxford don. This is something we weren't aware of before. Stalker is not just some Zone fundamentalist—he's a big reader. I bet there are copies of *Tragic Sense of Life, Wisdom and Insecurity, The Prelude* and everything else mentioned in the course of this summary. Who knows, maybe he even has some of Writer's books.* Stalker is in an exhausted rage about the lack of belief of Writer and Professor, not only these two but everyone like them. He thumps the hard floor and his wife, kindly now, tells him not to get overexcited, to go to bed. It's damp here, she says. If she only knew! Compared with where he's been this is as warm as toast! But yes, he sure looks tired. By anyone's standards it's been a long and damp day or lifetime—whichever is the longer or damper. A cuckoo clock chirrups the hour—as though

---

* In a sense Stalker's book collection is also Tarkovsky's: 'Only that which I would like to have in my home has the right to find itself in a shot of one of my films,' he said in an interview. 'If the objects are not to my liking, I simply cannot allow myself to leave them in the film.' (Bresson puts the emphasis on the things themselves: 'Make the objects look as if they want to be there.')

Stalker had brought back a souvenir from one of his previous trips to the Zone; or perhaps it was a gift from a
satisfied client.* She helps him into bed, taking off his
trousers and shoes. As before, he keeps his sweater on—
his sweater, which is dirty, soaking and stinky-looking,
ripe for the starring role in an advertisement for the latest breakthrough in biological detergents. She tucks him
in, sits on the side of the bed like she is looking after a
patient, giving him a tablet and water. Some blossom or
fluff is floating through the air, the same fluff or blossom
that was seen floating through the Zone, in the moments
after the land rippled like an acid trip so that the home
is suffused with magic. Stalker looked a bit Nosferatu-
like before, back in the Zone; now, in bed, he looks like
Nosferatu as the sun is about to come up. He's in that
exhausted, almost hysterical state that causes you to get
more and more worked up over things you can do noth-

---

* It's also further evidence of what Tarkovsky said about
only using things in his films that he would have in his own
house: the same cuckoo clock puts in an audio appearance
in *Mirror* when the children run out of the house to see
the fire.

ing about. All they can think about, he says, is not selling themselves cheap, how to get paid for every breath they take. No one believes. Not only those two—Writer and Professor, he means—no one. Who am I going to take there? He's on the brink—or in the grips—of a total emotional and nervous breakdown, tormented by what seems now not so much as a lack in others as his own excess of belief. The worst thing is, not only do they not believe in the Zone, no one even needs it. A devastating possibility: the most wonderful place, the most wonderful thing in the world, and no one even needs it. Effectively people have no need of what they most want, have learned to do without. We see his face and her hand, mopping him, consoling him even though he is inconsolable.

When Coetzee found himself 'sobbing uncontrollably' on reading *The Brothers Karamazov* he asked himself why he found himself 'more and more vulnerable' to those pages. It had nothing to do with ethics or politics and everything to do with 'the accents of anguish, the personal anguish of a soul unable to bear the horrors of this world.'

Back in the Zone Stalker said he might move there with his wife and child; now he tells his wife he won't even go there again. Talk about cutting off your nose to spite your face. Or maybe the unbearable horrors of this world have proved more bearable than the promise and refuge of the Zone. She says she'll go there with him.* After all, she reminds him, there are plenty of things she could wish for. Such as? That her husband wasn't a Stalker for one. That he wasn't so obsessed by this wretched Zone, that he would stop sleeping in his dirty sweater . . . you name it. There's also the possibility that she has realized that the one thing worse than his sneaking off to the Zone every chance he gets is having him here, getting under her feet, moping around at home the whole time. But no, she can't go there. Because she's a woman? No. Because what if she went and it didn't work for her either? A last straw,

---

* A lovely offer, reminiscent of the one my mum once made on behalf of my dad. Owing to an unlucky turn of events at school I seemed, in the sixth form, to have no friends. I had no one to go to the pub with and my mum said that my dad would go out for a drink with me, an idea I knew would not appeal to him as it would have involved spending money, which he hated, and going to the pub, which he never liked.

too terrible even to contemplate clutching. He turns his head to sleep.

THE TRAIN WHISTLES are blowing. Stalker's wife walks towards the wall and then sits down, turns to the camera and takes a cigarette from her packet. A dreadful moment, this, for me. By lighting and smoking a cigarette she turns herself, instantly, into something hideous. That sheepskin coat, we realize now, must stink of cigarettes— and her hair. And it's not just that: I hate all gestures associated with finding, lighting and smoking a cigarette.

Her family were against their marrying, she says. Everyone in the neighbourhood laughed at him. She has lit her cigarette and shakes the match to extinguish it. I hate that smell, the smell of an extinguished match, as much as I hate the smell of cigarette smoke and I also hate the sight—by the side of cookers without a self-ignition facility—of curled and blackened matches. Lots of creaking and groaning of timbers, and the usual drop and drip of a tap or a leak, all imparting a touch of the nautical to this homely scene. He was a Stalker, an eternal prisoner. She knew this about him, and about the kind of children Stalkers have. But still, when he said come with me she went, like an apostle, and she's never regretted it, not even with the pain and shame and sorrow.

Tarkovsky thought the wife's expression of love and devotion was the 'final miracle', the heart of the film, its ultimate lesson: 'namely that human love alone is—miraculously—proof against the blunt assertion that there is no hope for the world. This is our common, and incontrovertibly positive possession.' Well, as Philip Larkin said on discovering that he was 'too selfish, withdrawn and easily bored to love': 'useful to get that learned.' As a lesson this—like so much in *Sculpting in Time*—fails to do justice to the revealed complexity of what takes place on-screen, but it does correspond with Olga Surkova's assessment of Tarkovsky's second wife, Larissa, as 'a Russian angel standing guard over the persecuted Russian artist.'*

---

* That Tarkovsky intended something like this—Stalker and his wife as stand-ins for his own sense of persecuted devotion—seems especially likely given that he wanted Larissa to play the part but was dissuaded by Rerberg and co., who lobbied successfully for Alisa Freindlikh. Her to-camera monologue was originally intended to go at the beginning; only late in the process of shooting the third version did Tarkovsky decide to put it here, as a kind of epilogue.

At least that's how things started out. Then Larissa came to believe she was 'the fountain from which he drank'.

But of course in the film the wife is not married to a world-famous director, one of the most revered film-makers ever to have shouted 'Action', she's married to a Stalker whose pyjamas are his sweater.

Even with all the pain she has no regrets about the choice she made. In fact, it wouldn't have been any better

---

While Tarkovsky may have seen himself as a Stalker—a persecuted martyr taking us on voyages into a Zone where ultimate truths are revealed—he also became identified with the destination itself. There is a poignant moment in an interview with the terminally ill production designer Rashit Safiullin, who, when asked about the Zone, recalls the time he spent living, working and talking with Tarkovsky: 'Here you live being your inmost self . . . it's somewhere where you can talk with somebody, something unfathomable.' The interviewer asks him to clarify. Does he mean . . . ? 'Yes, speaking with god. When Andrei was no more I was bereaved of a person with whom I could talk about the most important things. That room vanished.' 'So he was the Room to you?' asks the interviewer. 'Yes.'

without the pain because then there would not have been any happiness. Without the pain there wouldn't have been any hope. Hmm. Except happiness trumps hope, at least in the short term. It's not just that if you're happy you have no need of hope. When you're happy, hope, like all the other big questions—as Solonitsyn's character, Sartorius, says in *Solaris*—becomes meaningless. It is possible, in parts of California particularly, to live a life devoid of hope (in what's to come) and brim full of happiness (for what is here now). Elsewhere, hope has persistence and endurance on its side, is happy to stand around and wait—for things to get bad again, for happiness to pass. In terms of the Zone, Stalker may have been right about his wife; maybe it wouldn't have worked for her there. She clings to hope and the Zone, he suspects, lets through those who've lost all hope. Life is shit. You put up with it. You hope even though you don't believe in hope. People who've got over terrible things say they never gave up hope, never stopped hoping. But hope is a source of torment as well as an inspiration. Didn't the Buddha counsel against hope? Wasn't hope one of the torments of Samsara from which we had to free ourselves? Besides, the Zone—on the evidence of this excursion at least—is not a place of hope so much as a place where hope turns in on itself, resigns itself to the way things are. To that extent she is there already, in the Zone.

MONKEY, IN PROFILE and in colour, still wearing that autumnal gold-brown headscarf, reading. Reading in the way people used to read, before there were so many books that they became a bit of a nuisance and burden, before there was even an inkling of the Kindle. Smoke is drifting. Nice-looking smoke, incense. Floating blossom. The loud cheep and chirrup of birds: Zone sounds, Zone blossom. But also the railroad and dockside moan of horns—sounds that were nowhere to be heard in the Zone, the quietest place on earth. We are on the brink, here, of one of the all-redeeming moments of any art form. It can't be isolated from what has gone before, it gathers into itself the whole film. But by 'all-redeeming' I don't just mean in the context of *this* film. It redeems, makes up for, every pointless bit of gore, every wasted special effect, all the stupidity in every film made before or since. Oh well, you think, none of that matters, all of that is worth it, for this. As we have seen several times already in *Stalker,* there is nothing symbolic about what occurs. The camera simply shows what is happening. It retreats down the table, past a glass half full of what looks like porter or some kind of Soviet Coca-Cola that has gone completely flat or probably started out that way. And a couple of empty, opaque glasses. Monkey lays down the book as if she has been memorizing what she was reading—which turns out, or so the voice-over would have us believe, to be a love poem by Fyodor Tyutchev.*

There is the moan of transport outside. She bends her head and looks at the glass with the flat cola in it and, evidently in response to her thoughts, the glass begins to move down the table. The dog whimpers and whines, aware he is in the presence of something not normal, but it is nice to think that the dog is at ease with her, that she and the dog have each other for company.† She glances

---

* Bjork got the lyrics to her song 'The Dull Flame of Desire'—on the album *Volta*—from the English translation of this poem, acknowledging *Stalker* as the source.

† Extraordinary, the way that this film continues to creep into my life in the most unexpected ways. In the last several years I've taken to listening to ambient music—William Basinski, Stars of the Lid, that kind of stuff—while working (the drone, the lack of beat, is an aid to

at the dog, not unkindly, and the dog quietens down. It could be that she has zapped or silenced him with her telekinetic powers, but it seems more likely that he is reassured that nothing bad is happening here and can resume his nap or continue enjoying lying on the floor of his new home. She focuses her attention on the glasses once more. How was this done? Like doubting Thomas sticking his finger in the wound I want to know how this

---

concentration). I'd listened to the Lids' album *The Tired Sounds Of* dozens of times and had always liked the funny moment, on 'Requiem for Dying Mothers, part 2', when a dog starts whining (just as I'd liked the dog barking on one of the recordings of Dylan's 'Every Grain of Sand'). I assumed a dog had somehow strayed into the studio and the Lids had decided to retain the intrusion as a random bit of canine backing vocals. Then, listening to it as I was writing about this scene, I realized the sound of the dog whimpering was preceded by a slight scraping noise. I listened to it again. And again. There could be no doubt, there was nothing accidental about it: the Lids had *sampled* the sound of the dog whining in response to the glass moving along the table!

miracle was achieved. With a magnet hidden by the cola while someone under the table dragged it along?* Next she moves a jam jar with something in it, just a couple of inches. Then the big tall empty glass.†

---

* Apparently Tarkovsky personally dragged it with a piece of discreetly painted string.

† Sound recordist Vladimir Sharun gives a full account of how the film came to end like this: 'Thanks to Tarkovsky's passion for anything out of the ordinary a man called Eduard Naumov somehow ended up within our circle. . . . Once Naumov showed us one of his films. The film showed Ninel Sergeyevna Kulagina [who] discovered she had an ability for telekinesis—she moved objects with her sight. On the screen Kulagina, surrounded by a group of people looking like scientists, was sitting behind a table with a transparent top—to avoid any claims of forgery. On the table there was a lighter, a spoon, some other items. Kulagina's face darkened with exertion, she fixed her unblinking stare on the lighter which followed her gaze. Tarkovsky attentively watched Naumov's film and after it was finished he immediately exclaimed: "Well, what do you say, here is the ending for *Stalker!*"'

She rests her head on the table, brings the glass right
to the edge of the table before propelling it that extra,
gravity-grabbing centimetre. It falls over the edge. In
the story quoted earlier, Oë writes that 'one of the glasses
that's moved to the edge of the table falls to the floor and
breaks into pieces. Up to this point you saw the child's
face behind the glass, so now you see it better, and the
expression on it appears to be savouring the sound of
destruction.'

Except the glass doesn't break. We don't see it break
and we don't hear it break either. What we hear, in fact,
is the glass *not* breaking. It hits the floor not with a smash
and tinkle but a sturdy, almost indestructible crash. The
claim that the child is 'savouring' the destruction—that,
to judge by her eyes, she is 'harbouring some kind of
malevolent force', that she might even be 'the antichrist'
whose role is 'to destroy everything'—is a further projection intended to confirm the initial misreading, or mis-
hearing. These particulars aside, Oë's reading of the scene
is completely out of whack with the larger scheme of the
film. Would he really have us believe that Stalker was
rewarded for his faith by a daughter who was not only
crippled but a malevolent, glass-smashing antichrist to

boot? Her telekinetic powers, surely, are a manifestation of unmeasurable compensation or consolation.

The thing in the jam jar, we can see now, is an eggshell or the remains of one, but at this late stage we are untroubled by any irritable straining after symbolic meaning and significance. There's just a jar with an eggshell in it and Monkey's head in that autumnal-gold scarf, resting on the table as if it's a pillow. It's impossible to say with any certainty what the look in her eyes and on her face mean. She seems content, almost drowsy in the knowledge of her harmless power.

A train is approaching, making the windows rattle, making the jar shake and the table too, as it did right at the beginning, when she was asleep in bed with her mum and dad, before he went to the Zone and got her a nice doggy. The vibrations from the train are so strong that her head is being shaken as it rumbles and rattles past, blaring out Beethoven's 'Ode to Joy'. Eventually the noise diminishes and the train passes and there is just the rattle of the train that has passed and her eyes, her watching eyes, and her face and head, resting on the table, watching us watching her, fading to black.

Or was it possibly nothing more than a fundamentally recognizable genre all the while, no matter what Writer averred?

Nothing more or less than a read?

—David Markson, *This Is Not a Novel*

FILMS BY TARKOVSKY

The Steamroller and the Violin (1960)
Ivan's Childhood (1962)
Andrei Rublev (1969)
Solaris (1972)
Mirror (1974)
Stalker (1979)
Tempo di Viaggio (1980)
Nostalghia (1983)
The Sacrifice (1986)

DOCUMENTARIES ABOUT—
AND FILMIC HOMAGES TO—TARKOVSKY

Moscow Elegy, directed by Aleksandr Sokurov, 1987.
One Day in the Life of Andrei Arsenevich, directed by Chris Marker, 2000.
Rerberg and Tarkovsky: The Reverse Side of 'Stalker', directed by Igor Maiboroda, 2008.
Ajapeegel, directed by Jeremy Millar, 2008.

BOOKS BY TARKOVSKY

Sculpting in Time, translated by Kitty Hunter-Blair (London: Bodley Head, 1986).
Time Within Time: The Diaries 1970–86, translated by Kitty Hunter-Blair (London: Faber & Faber, 1994).
Collected Screenplays, translated by William Powell and Natasha Synessios (London: Faber & Faber, 1999).
Instant Light: Tarkovsky Polaroids, edited by Giovanni Chiarmonte and Andrey A. Tarkovsky (London: Thames and Hudson, 2004).

BOOKS ABOUT TARKOVSKY

Robert Bird, *Andrei Tarkovsky: Elements of Cinema* (London: Reaktion, 2008).

Nathan Dunne (ed.), *Tarkovsky* (London: Black Dog, 2008).

John Gianvito (ed.), *Andrei Tarkovsky Interviews* (Jackson: University Press of Mississippi, 2006).

Vida T. Johnson and Graham Petrie, *The Films of Andrei Tarkovsky: A Visual Fugue* (Bloomington: Indiana University Press, 1994).

Mark Le Fanu, *The Cinema of Andrei Tarkovsky* (London: BFI, 1987).

Marina Tarkovskaya (ed.), *About Andrei Tarkovsky: Memoirs and Biographies* (Moscow: Progress Publishing, 1990).

WEBSITE

http://www.nostalghia.com

Notes

There are some unacknowledged quotations and misquotations in the text. Sources for these are listed here, along with the ones that were conventionally presented.

7 'THE WORST OF HIS FILMS,' etc.: interview with Maria Chugnova in Tarkovsky, *Time Within Time*, p. 357.

8 'A RING AT THE DOOR': Edmond and Jules de Goncourt, *Pages from the Goncourt Journals*, edited by Robert Baldick (New York: NYRB Classics, 2007), p. 40.

9 'IF THE REGULAR LENGTH': quoted by Vladimir Goldstein in Nathan Dunne (ed.), *Tarkovsky*, p. 188.

12 'A LITTLE MORE DYNAMIC': quoted by Evgeny Tsymbal in Dunne, ibid., p. 351.

15 'I THINK THAT': Tarkovsky, *Sculpting in Time*, p. 63.

15 'NINETY MINUTES OF SITTING': Richard Price, *Clockers* (London: Bloomsbury, 2003; first published 1992), p. 28.

17 'THE WORLD OUTSIDE': Anne Applebaum, *Gulag: A History* (New York: Doubleday, 2003), p. xxix.

17 'A WAY OF LIFE': Tony Judt, *Postwar* (London: Heinemann, 2005), p. 323.

18 'THE SOVIET REPRESSIVE SYSTEM': Applebaum, *Gulag*, p. xvi.

19 'HE'S SUCH A': Mick Jagger, quoted in Peter Doggett, *There's a Riot Going On* (Edinburgh: Canongate, 2007), p. 211.

24 'TOTALLY OUT OF IT': Vladimir Sharun, interview at nostalghia.com.

27 'A MAN'S WORK': Albert Camus, *Selected Essays and Notebooks* (Harmondsworth: Penguin, 1984), p. 26.

28 'MEN SWAGGERING INTO SALOONS': Don DeLillo, *Libra* (New York: Viking, 1988), p. 17.

29 'A BOOK ABOUT NOTHING': *The Letters of Gustave Flaubert 1830–1857*, edited by Francis Steegmuller (Cambridge, Mass.: Harvard University Press, 1980), p. 154.

33 'RIGHT IN THE EYES': Roland Barthes, *The Responsibility of Forms* (New York: Hill and Wang, 1985), p. 242.

36 'DID NOT MAKE *SOLARIS*': Stanislaw Lem, quoted in Robert Bird, *Andrei Tarkovsky: Elements of Cinema,* p. 116.

45 'ON THE THRESHOLD': Roberto Calasso, *K.* (New York: Knopf, 2005), p. 10.

46 'SOMEONE EMBARKS': Billy Collins, *Sailing Around the Room* (New York: Random House, 2001), p. 158.

49 'BEGAN TO MAKE FILMS': Ingmar Bergman, quoted in *Rerberg and Tarkovsky: The Reverse Side of 'Stalker'* (film).

49 'USING SOME OF HIS TYPICAL': Wim Wenders, *The Act of Seeing* (London: Faber & Faber, 1997), p. 42.

54 'TO BEGIN TWO CONSECUTIVE': Anthony Hecht, quoted in Christopher Ricks, *True Friendship* (New Haven: Yale University Press, 2010), p. 95.

55 'HAPPY THE HARE': *The English Auden,* edited by Edward Mendelson (London: Faber & Faber, 1977), p. 283.

58 'MAKE VISIBLE WHAT': Robert Bresson, *Notes on the Cinematographer* (London: Quartet Books, 1986), pp. 72, 81.

61 ROAD TRIP: I got the story about Tarkovsky and the road trip through Utah from Tom Luddy himself. It is broadly corroborated by Zanussi's reminiscences in Marina Tarkovskaya (ed.), *About Andrei Tarkovsky: Memoirs and Biographies,* pp. 210–15.

64 'THE UNHOMELY': Martin Heidegger, *Introduction to Metaphysics* (New Haven: Yale University Press, 2000), p. 161.

65 'RASHIT, THE FLOWERS': Georgi Rerberg in *Rerberg and Tarkovsky: The Reverse Side of 'Stalker'* (film).

70 AN AMAZING PLACE . . . IS NORMAL HERE: slightly adapted from Roberto Calasso, *Ka* (New York: Knopf, 1998), p. 165.

71 'PUTTING ITSELF IN A PERSONAL RELATION': William James, *The Varieties of Religious Experience: A Study in Human Nature* (New York: The Modern Library, 1999; first published 1902), p. 506.

72 'SOBBING UNCONTROLLABLY': J. M. Coetzee, *Diary of a Bad Year* (London: Harvill Secker, 2007), p. 223.

73 'THIS IS WHAT EXISTS': Max Frisch, quoted in Hans Magnus Enzensberger, *Civil War* (London: Granta, 1994), p. 78.

75 ROBERT POLIDORI and JONAS BENDIKSEN: see, respectively, *Zones of Exclusion* (Göttingen, Germany: Steidl, 2003) and *Satellites* (New York: Aperture, 2006).

76 'WHAT CONFERS ON IT': Slavoj Žižek, 'The Thing from Inner Space'. It seems there are various different versions of this essay floating around. The one quoted from here can be found at http://www.lacan.com/zizekthing.htm (September 1999).

77 'THEY FED IT': for German original, see *The Selected Poetry of Rainer Maria Rilke,* edited by Stephen Mitchell (New York: Vintage International, 1989), p. 240. Translation by Shaun Whiteside.

78 SCIENTISTS WHO CARRIED OUT: http://www.bbc.co.uk/news/science-environment-10819027.

79 'BEYOND A CERTAIN POINT': quoted in Roberto Calasso, *K.* (New York: Knopf, 2005), p. 20. This translation suited me better than Michael Hofmann's in *Zürau Aphorisms* (New York: Schocken, 2006), p. 7.

81 'FEEL . . . THAT THE ZONE': Tarkovsky, *Sculpting in Time,* p. 200.

82 'ONCE I WAS A MAN': Maurice Merleau-Ponty, *Phenomenology of Perception* (London: Routledge Classics, 2002,), pp. 329–30.

84 NOT A SET OF EVENTS: adapted from David Abram, *The Spell of the Sensuous* (New York: Vintage, 1997), p. 193. I am indebted to Abram more generally for my discussion of the Zone and the sudden gust of wind in this section.

84 'HAS NO MEANING IN ITSELF': Milan Kundera, *Immortality* (London: Faber & Faber, 1991), pp. 249–50.

91 'SHOULD DOUBT . . . THE EXISTENCE': Tarkovsky, interview with Guerra at nostalghia.com.

91 'THE IMAGE BECOMES': Tarkovsky, *Sculpting in Time,* p. 68.

92 'OVER AND OVER': *Andrei Tarkovsky Interviews,* edited by John Gianvito, p. 42.

93 'A LIFE OF WHICH THE KEYNOTE': William James, *The Varieties of Religious Experience,* p. 572.

103 'SUDDENLY ONE OF': Vladimir Sharun, interview at nostalghia.com.

103 'TOTAL DISASTER': Tarkovsky, *Time Within Time,* p. 146.

104 'A RIGID IDEA': Evgeny Tsymbal in Dunne, *Tarkovsky,* p. 344.

105 'EVERYTHING IS GOING TO BE DIFFERENT': Tarkovsky, *Time Within Time,* p. 146.

105 'HE COULD NOT UNDERSTAND': Vladimir Sharun, interview at nostalghia.com.

105 'KALASHNIKOV REFUSED' and 'HE DIDN'T HAVE THE GUTS': Tarkovsky, *Time Within Time,* pp. 154 and 151.

105 'ALMOST VISUALLY IDENTICAL': Maria Chugunova, quoted by Tsymbal, in Dunne, *Tarkovsky,* p. 350.

105 'LACKED SIMPLICITY': Ibid.

106 'LIGHTWEIGHT SHALLOW PEOPLE': Tarkovsky, *Time Within Time,* p. 145.

106 'FOR BEHAVING LIKE A BASTARD': Ibid., p. 154.

106 'BUT AT THE COST': from *Rerberg and Tarkovsky: Reverse Side of 'Stalker'* (film).

107 'A CORPSE': Tarkovsky, *Time Within Time,* p. 146.

108 'INVINCIBLE': *Andrei Tarkovsky Interviews,* edited by John Gianvito, p. 125.

108 'YOU ARE DISTINGUISHED': Alexander Galich, quoted in Lesley Chamberlain, *Motherland* (London: Atlantic, 2004), p. 36.

111 'THE SINGLE MOST IMPORTANT': Robert Bird, *Andrei Tarkovsky,* p. 57.

112 'THERE REALLY IS': Arkady and Boris Strugatsky, *Roadside Picnic* (London: Gollancz, 2007; translation first published 1977), p. 29.

113 'UP THE RIVER': Vladimir Sharun, interview at nostalghia.com.

115 'TO EVERY NATURAL': Wordsworth, from *The Prelude: A Parallel Text,* edited by J. C. Maxwell (Harmondsworth: Penguin, 1972), p. 108.

117 'I SEE AROUND ME': *The Selected Poetry and Prose of Wordsworth,* edited by Geoffrey Hartman (New York: Signet Classics, 1970), p. 50.

118 'THE THEN IS CONSTANTLY REPEATED': Thomas Mann, *The Magic Mountain* (New York: Vintage, 1996), p. 339.

121 'SOME KIND OF DRUG DEALER': Tarkovsky, *Time Within Time,* p. 147.

122 'WHERE ART IS DYING': Milan Kundera, *Encounter* (London: Faber & Faber, 2010), p. 146.

129 'IF AT THE END': quoted in Robert Bird, *Andrei Tarkovsky,* p. 163.

132 'EVERYTHING ON EARTH': Ibid., p. 142.

132 'PERHAPS WE ARE *HERE*': for German original, see *The Selected Poetry of Rainer Maria Rilke,* edited by Stephen Mitchell, pp. 198–200. Translation by Shaun Whiteside.

133 'CAME TO FEEL': Lesley Chamberlain, *Motherland,* p. 264.

136 'IN THE RIVER': *Andrei Tarkovsky Interviews,* edited by John Gianvito, p. 27.

137 NOTHING ON THE WALLS BUT DAMP: adapted from Wisława

Szymborska's poem 'Cave', in *Poems New and Collected 1957–1997* (London: Faber & Faber, 1999), p. 103.

138 'UTTERLY NEW TERRAIN': Wim Wenders, *The Act of Seeing*, p. 42.

138 'THE DARKNESS GREW LOUD': William Langewiesche, *American Ground: The Unbuilding of the World Trade Center* (New York: North Point, 2002), pp. 28–29.

138 'SHOOTING IS GOING OUT': Robert Bresson, *Notes on the Cinematographer*, p. 94.

142 'I SAW TARKOVSKY'S *STALKER*': Tilda Swinton, http://www.movie line.com/2009/05/tilda-swinton-i-think-youve-got-the-wrong -person.php.

144 'THERE OUGHT TO BE IN PARIS': Robert Bresson, *Notes on the Cinematographer*, p. 117.

145 'FROM WHERE ELSE': John Berger, *Keeping a Rendezvous* (Harmondsworth: Granta, 1992), p. 14.

149 'ENTIRE LIFE HAS CONSISTED': Tarkovsky, quoted in Robert Bird, *Andrei Tarkovsky*, p. 47.

154 'SUBSEQUENT FILM': Tarkovsky, *Time Within Time*, p. 169.

158 'I'M REDUCED TO': Tarkovsky, *Sculpting in Time*, p. 200.

158 'A TEST': ('that results in a man either withstanding or breaking. Whether a man survives or not depends on his sense of individual worth, his ability to distinguish what is important from what is transitory.'): Tarkovsky, quoted in Robert Bird, *Andrei Tarkovsky*, p. 69.

159 'AN INFINITE, IF DANK ENCLOSURE': David Thomson, *Have You Seen . . . ?* (London: Allen Lane, 2008), p. 822.

163 'THE BELIEVER WILL OPEN': Alan Watts, *The Wisdom of Insecurity* (New York: Pantheon, 1951), p. 24.

164 'IS FAITH IN HOPE': Miguel de Unamuno, *Tragic Sense of Life* (New York: Dover, 1954), p. 200.

165 'PEOPLE WILL DO ANYTHING': Carl Jung, *Psychology and Alchemy* (London: Routledge & Kegan Paul, 1953), p. 99.

174 'THE EYE WANTS TO SLEEP': James Tate, 'Absences', *Selected Poems* (Manchester: Carcanet, 1997), p. 106.

176 'MY DISCOVERY': Ingmar Bergman, at nostalghia.com.

177 'EVERY TIME IT WAS': Safiullin, interview, bonus extra, on *Stalker* DVD.

177 'THE GREATER THE DEGREE,' ETC.: Nadezhda Mandelstam, *Hope Against Hope: A Memoir*, translated by Max Hayward (London: Harvill, 1999; first published 1971), p. 92.

NOTES TO PAGES 180–216

180 'THE POINT OF ROOMS': Don DeLillo, *White Noise* (London: Picador, 1985), p. 305.

182 'EACH ONE OF US': John Berger and Nella Bielski, *A Question of Geography* (London: Faber & Faber, 1987), p. 48.

184 'I COMPLETELY AGREE': Tarkovsky, from an interview with Aldo Tassone at nostalghia.com. Translated slightly differently in *Andrei Tarkovsky Interviews,* edited by John Gianvito, p. 61; 'THE ZONE DOESN'T': interview with Laurence Cossé, ibid., p. 169.

189 'EVERYTHING, AFTER PASSING THROUGH': Miguel de Unamuno, *Tragic Sense of Life,* p. 201. (In the English edition—translated from the Spanish—the first use of 'film' is given as 'cinematograph show'; hence the change!)

201 'THE EXCELLENT ACTING OF THE DOG': Kenzaburo Oë, *A Quiet Life* (London: Picador, 1998), p. 92.

201 'PLANTS AND ANIMALS': Bélas Balázs, quoted in Robert Bird, *Andrei Tarkovsky,* p. 70.

201 'POSING': Donatas Banionis, quoted in Bird, ibid., p. 75.

202 'FANTASTIC DOG': Knyazhinsky, interview, bonus extra, on *Stalker* DVD.

204 'ONLY THAT WHICH': Tarkovsky, interview with Guerra at nostalghia.com.

204 'MAKE THE OBJECTS LOOK': Robert Bresson, *Notes on the Cinematographer,* p. 101.

209 'FINAL MIRACLE': Tarkovsky, *Sculpting in Time,* pp. 198–99.

209 'TOO SELFISH': Philip Larkin, 'Wild Oats', *Collected Poems* (London: Faber & Faber, 1988), p. 143.

209 'A RUSSIAN ANGEL': Olga Surhova, quoted in *Rerberg and Tarkovsky: The Reverse Side of 'Stalker'* (film).

210 'HERE YOU LIVE': Rashit Safiullin, interview, bonus extra, on *Stalker* DVD.

215 'THANKS TO TARKOVSKY'S': Vladimir Sharun, interview at nostalghia.com.

216 'ONE OF THE GLASSES'; Kenzaburo Oë, 'The Guide *(Stalker)*', in *A Quiet Life,* pp. 87 and 90.

Acknowledgments

I would like to thank Mark Cousins, Tom Luddy and Chris Mitchell for reading an early version of the manuscript and making helpful suggestions and corrections. I am particularly grateful to Tom for furnishing me with information about Tarkovsky's trip to Telluride.

A few passages from this book first appeared, in very different form, in the *Guardian*. I am grateful to Michael Hann for commissioning and publishing that piece.

ABOUT THE AUTHOR

Geoff Dyer is the author of *Jeff in Venice, Death in Varanasi* and three previous novels, as well as many nonfiction books including *The Ongoing Moment* (winner of the International Center of Photography's Infinity Award for writing on photography), *But Beautiful* (winner of the Somerset Maugham Award), *Out of Sheer Rage* (a finalist for a National Book Critics Circle Award), and, most recently, *Otherwise Known as the Human Condition,* a collection of essays. He is the recipient of the American Academy of Arts and Letters' E. M. Forster Award and a Lannan Literary Fellowship. Dyer lives in London.